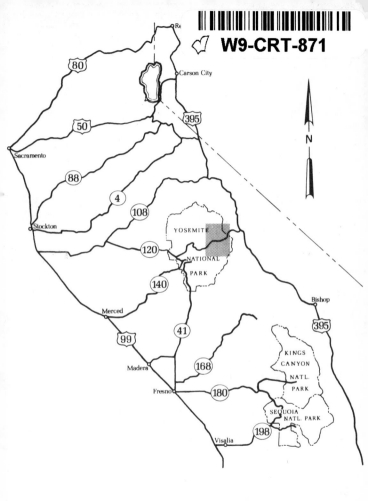

Location of the TUOLUMNE MEADOWS quadrangle

High Sierra
Hiking Guide #4

TUOLUMNE
MEADOWS

a complete guide
to the Meadows
and surrounding uplands,
including descriptions of
more than 100 miles of trails

by Jeffrey P. Schaffer
and Thomas Winnett

Wilderness Press

BERKELEY

ACKNOWLEDGMENTS

I am grateful to the following individuals who have helped to improve this guidebook. Ronald M. Mackie, Jr., the Chief Backcountry Ranger, shared Park philosophy and management problems with me and gave me a *carte blanche* that enabled me to do unrestricted field work in the Park, including a six-week task of resurveying the topographic map of this area. David Graber, who is probably *the* Yosemite bear expert, provided valuable information on bear life and bear problems, and he reviewed the subchapter on this matter. Reviewing the geology chapter were Prof. Samuel P. Welles, of the Paleontology Department at the University of California, Berkeley, and Paul Bateman, of the U.S. Geological Survey, Menlo Park. Carl W. Sharsmith, of the Yosemite Natural History Association and rightfully a legend in his own time, increased my biological awareness and at campfires shared his vast knowledge about the Park's history and natural history.

–Jeffrey P. Schaffer

First printing 1970
Second printing 1971
Revised third printing 1973
SECOND EDITION 1977

Copyright © 1977 by Jeffrey P. Schaffer and Thomas Winnett

Map by Jeffrey P. Schaffer

Photos by the authors

Library of Congress Card Catalog No. 77-70562

International Standard Book No. 911824-59-6

Manufactured in the United States

Published by Wilderness Press
2440 Bancroft Way
Berkeley CA 94704

Introduction

THE HIGH SIERRA HIKING GUIDES published by Wilderness Press are the first complete guides to the famous High Sierra. Each guide covers at least one 15-minute USGS topographic quadrangle, an area about 14 miles east-west by 17 miles north-south. The first page inside the front cover shows the location of the quadrangle covered by this guidebook.

There is a great and increasing demand for literature about America's favorite wilderness, John Muir's "Range of Light." To meet this demand, we have undertaken this guide series. The purpose of each book in the series is threefold: first, to provide a reliable basis for planning a trip; second, to serve as a field guide while you are on the trail; and third, to stimulate you to further field investigation and background reading. In each guide there are a minimum of 100 miles of described trails, and the descriptions are supplemented with maps, mileages and natural history. HIGH SIERRA HIKING GUIDES are based on first-hand observation. There is absolutely no substitute for walking the trails, so for this guide we walked and mapped all the trails.

In planning this series, we used the 15-minute quadrangle as the unit because—though every way of dividing the Sierra is arbitrary—the quadrangle map is the chosen aid of almost every wilderness traveler. Inside the back cover of this book is an original, accurate map of the quadrangle, showing all described trails. With this map, you can always get where you want to go, with a minimum of detours or wasted effort. (Additional copies of the map can be bought separately from Wilderness Press or its dealers.)

To camp overnight in the Yosemite wilderness, you will need a wilderness permit. In Tuolumne Meadows the Information Center dispenses only information, not wilderness permits. Permits are obtainable at a booth in the parking lot near the west end of the Tuolumne Meadows Lodge spur road, which leaves Highway 120 just ½ mile east of the bridge over the Tuolumne River. From late June through the Labor Day weekend this booth is open on Friday nights, and it opens as early as 6 a.m. on Saturdays. In the spring you can get a permit for a backcountry trip by writing, between Feb. 1 and May 31, to: Backcountry Office, P.O. Box 577, Yosemite National Park CA 95389. In obtaining a permit in person or by mail, you must state what trailhead you will leave from, when, and where you will camp each night. Only a certain number of backpackers are allowed to backpack in from a given trailhead on a given day. Permits obtained in person are available on a first-come-first-served basis up to 24 hours before your departure time.

Several other regulations are of interest to backpackers: 1) Wood fires are prohibited above 9600 feet elevation. 2) Camping is not permitted within 25 feet of any trail or body of water. 3) Camping is not permitted within 4 trail miles of Tuolumne Meadows, Glacier Point or the rim of Yosemite Valley. 4) Maximum size of a camping group is 25. 5) Pets are not allowed on trails in the backcountry.

Unicorn Peak from Soda Springs

Contents

The Country

WHETHER THE VISITOR to Tuolumne Meadows country comes merely to look or whether he comes to experience, the country will claim him. This wonderland rich in geological history boasts a genial climate and an abundance of trails, which are an open invitation to the most casual visitor to discover for himself what lies beyond the noise and tourism of Yosemite Valley. In the meadows, the car camper and the resort sojourner will find their requisites—if on a rather modest scale. On the heights above the meadow the hiker will find solitude, and in this solitude he will come to know why wilderness preserves like these are so necessary to man.

Tuolumne Meadows is the largest subalpine meadow in the High Sierra, 2½ miles long and ½ mile wide. Here the Lyell Fork and the Dana Fork of the Tuolumne River commingle their snow-fed waters and meander through the wide meadows. The waters of these placid pools then leap down a series of spectacular falls into the Grand Canyon of the Tuolumne, one of the deepest canyons on earth.

The Tuolumne River, manipulated by man to be the slaker of San Francisco's thirst, rises in a thousand snow fields and a dozen glaciers along the Sierra crest. Its drainage embraces most of the quadrangle, but two other streams drain portions of the quad. The southwest quarter of the area, beyond the Cathedral Range, is Merced River drainage: that water flows through Yosemite Valley. The northeast corner, beyond the Sierra crest, is Lee Vining Creek drainage: that water courses down into Mono Lake and evaporates from this inland alkaline sea.

Just one road crosses the quadrangle: Highway 120, the Tioga Road. The road leaves Yosemite Park at Tioga Pass, the highest automobile pass in California, and the only place to cross the Sierra by auto between here and Walker Pass, several hundred miles south.

But while there is only one road in this quad, there are two master trails, and they meet in the heart of the quad. The famous John Muir Trail, coming up from Yosemite Valley, enters on the southwest and ascends Sunrise Creek, drops down to the meadows and proceeds east, then turns southeast up the Lyell Fork to the southeast corner of the quad, bound for Mt. Whitney. The less famous Tahoe-Yosemite Trail begins at the Tuolumne Soda Springs, in the meadows, leads west to Glen Aulin, and then heads north up Cold Canyon, bound for Meeks Bay on Lake Tahoe. The increasingly popular tri-state Pacific Crest Trail is routed along the Muir trail southeast of the meadows and along the Tahoe-Yosemite Trail northwest of them.

Besides these master trails there are several hundred miles of other main trails and side trails, many of them not shown on the USGS topo map—but all shown on the map in this book. These trails penetrate the forests and probe the high country, so that those who like to spend their time in timber have plenty of choices of campsites, and so do those for whom the alpine country above timberline is endlessly compelling. One very popular trail—actually, a sequence of connecting trails—is the High Sierra Loop Trail, which links the backcountry High Sierra Camps (see the Chapter "The Camps"). The full loop includes Glen Aulin and May Lake; an abbreviated loop embraces only Vogelsang, Merced Lake and Sunrise.

For the naturalist, there are over 500 species of vascular plants to look for and identify, making the meadows one of the finest centers for subalpine botanizing in California. The meadows are also a summer home to forty-some kinds of birds and more than twenty species of mammals. Those interested in alpine plants will find easily accessible alpine slopes on Mt. Dana and the Dana Plateau, just east of Tioga Pass and Tioga Lake, respectively, and along the Tioga Crest, in this quadrangle's northeast corner.

The History

TUOLUMNE MEADOWS, like the United States, was discovered by Indians. They used a trans-Sierra route through the meadows perhaps as early as 2500 B.C., for purposes of trade, west-slope Miwoks trading with east-slope Monos.

This route, the Mono Trail, led from Yosemite Valley past Tenaya Lake through Tuolumne Meadows, over the Sierra crest at Mono Pass and down Bloody Canyon to Mono Lake. In October 1833 Joseph Walker and his men followed part of this route on the first east-west crossing of the Sierra by white men. Walker and his party were the first white men to see Yosemite Valley, glimpsing it from the north rim.

In the early 1850's, soon after California became a state, a war of extermination against the Yosemite Indians began. The Indians lost. In the last episode of this campaign, Lt. Tredwell Moore, the ranking Army officer on the scene, ordered the execution of Chief Teneiya and the few other Indians remaining in the Valley. Somehow, they heard of the order, and fled eastward over the Mono Trail. Moore's men, in pursuit, became the first white men to see Tuolumne Meadows. They didn't find the Indians, but they spent some time in the high country exploring its canyons and upland slopes.

In 1860 the State Legislature appointed a group that became known as the Whitney Survey to map the state of California. In the summer of 1863, in Tuolumne Meadows, the survey party set up camp at the Soda Springs. From here they reconnoitered the area, climbed Mt. Dana and almost reached the top of Mt. Lyell, which they pronounced unclimbable. The expedition leader, William Brewer, wrote of the upper Lyell Fork that it was "picturesque, romantic. But prosy truth bids me to say that mosquitoes swarmed in myriads."

Five years later arrived the man who was to tell the world about Yosemite and the High Sierra: a Scottish sheepherder with the terse Scottish name of John Muir. He visited Yosemite briefly in 1868 and the next year he spent the whole summer in the High Sierra, herding sheep for a rancher. After rambling over the Tuolumne area he wrote:

> The best gains of this trip were the lessons of unity and inter-relation of all the features of the landscape revealed in general views . . . Every rock, mountain, stream, plant, lake, forest, garden, bird, beast, insect seems to call and invite us to come and learn something of its history and relationship.

In 1871 Muir, while somewhere among the peaks he called the "Merced Group," near the southeast corner of the *Tuolumne Meadows* quadrangle, was delighted to discover a glacier. Until then people had thought that all the Ice Age glaciers in the Sierra had melted, and for several years after, such geological authorities as J.D. Whitney and Clarence King denied there were glaciers in the Sierra.

Meanwhile, in 1864, Congress had granted Yosemite Valley and the Mariposa Grove of Big Trees to California as a natural preserve. But Muir felt that a much larger area should be preserved, and in the summer of 1889, over a campfire at the Soda Springs, he proposed to his companion the creation of a Yosemite National Park. His companion at the lodgepole-fueled warming fire was Robert Underwood Johnson, an editor of *Century Magazine*. Johnson put his influence, including his magazine, at the disposal of Muir and the park plan. In 1890 Congress created Yosemite National Park, with roughly its present borders.

After the bill passed, Yosemite was put under the supervision of the Army, and many raw recruits from eastern cities got their calluses on the backcountry trails of our quadrangle.

But long before people came to Tuolumne Meadows for recreation, they came to get rich quick. Early in 1860 a prospecting party scrambled over the summit looking for gold or silver in the Tioga Pass area. They found "the biggest silver ledge ever discovered" right at the crest north of Tioga Pass (see Day Hike #12). The news languished when more exciting finds were made east of here, near the Nevada border, and not until 1877 was the silver content proved out by assay. Then the rush was on. From 1878 to 1884 the area between upper Gaylor Lake and Shell Lake was overrun by miners, engineers, merchants, mule drivers and adventurers.

All this activity led to a plan for a road to the mines from the railhead at Copperopolis, near Angels Camp. A road already existed as far as Crocker's Station, about two miles west of the present Park entrance on Highway 120. In 1880 the officers of the mining company directed that a route be surveyed which would be good for both a wagon road and a railroad. The survey was completed in 1882, construction was begun eastward from Crocker's Station that year, and the wagon road was completed in September 1883.

Ten months later the mining company went broke and folded up operations; no ore ever moved down the Tioga Road. If that is ironic, it is a further irony that only eight years after construction began, Yosemite became a national park, and it is doubtful that anyone would have been allowed to build this road across a national park like Yosemite. If the park had been established prior to this mining activity, then present-day visitors would probably have to get to Tuolumne Meadows on a horse or afoot.

From 1890 to 1915 the road, though physically in the Park, remained a private enterprise, because when the federal gov-

Great Sierra Mine cabin

ernment created Yosemite National Park it did not buy the right-of-way. Numerous attempts to get Congress to appropriate the money all failed, and it took the ingenuity of Stephen T. Mather, soon to be the first director of the National Park Service, to put the road legally in the Park. Mather got Congress to pass a bill that would allow the government to accept the gift of things like the Tioga Road, and then got some wealthy friends to join him in buying the rights to the road. They gave the road to the Park in 1915.

The Park Service repaired the road and more or less kept it up, but it remained all dirt until 1937. In that year, a new, paved section from Fairview Dome to Tioga Pass was opened. In 1939 another one, from Crane Flat to White Wolf junction, was completed, and in 1961 the new central section, between these two sections, was finished.

Although Tuolumne Meadows has been acclaimed as a fine camping place since Lt. Moore's visit in 1852, very little development occurred there for many years after. Cabins were built in the 1850's and 1860's by sheepmen using the meadows for summer pasture, but they're long since gone. From about 1885 to 1895, John Lembert, who had homesteaded a plot at the Soda Springs, offered the tourist what hospitality and help he could.

Lembert died in 1896, and the homestead passed to two brothers, who sold it to the Sierra Club in 1912. The club maintained a campground for members and guests overlooking the river by the Soda Springs until 1972, when it gave the land to the Park Service. This campground was then used as a public walk-in campground until 1976, when it was closed to all camping.

The Curry Company public lodge on the Dana Fork was opened in 1916 by a predecessor company, which also maintained a tourist camp on the shore of Tenaya Lake where Murphy Creek flows in. The Curry Company moved this camp to May Lake in 1938, and later set up the store and cafe near the main campground in the meadows.

The Geology

THE VISITOR TO THE *Tuolumne Meadows* quadrangle today generally sees the impressive effects of glaciation upon the area's predominantly granitic rock. In other guides in this series we have stressed the abundance of this rock type and the importance of glaciation of it. In this book's geology chapter, however, we're going to take a different approach and stress that there have been many changes in this area's rocks, life and climate over a very long period of time. We don't mean to short-change granite and glaciation, so in the trail descriptions we often talk about granitic and glacial features.

The oldest rocks of the *Tuolumne Meadows* quadrangle date back to Ordovician or Silurian times—about 450 million years ago. Although this age is so remote that we really can't comprehend how long ago it was, the earth back then was already quite mature, having reached 90% of its present age. The physical and chemical processes that shape the earth's landscapes today were generally operating back then, and they resulted in the formation of rocks quite similar to those being formed today.

If we were to step into a time machine and travel back to the ancient Tuolumne Meadows area, we would see an amazingly different landscape. Instead of hiking in the mountains, we'd be swimming in a shallow sea inhabited by graptolites, trilobites and a great diversity of other invertebrates. The only vertebrates we'd see would be primitive, slow-moving, jawless fish. In this marine environment we would need to wear special survival suits, for oxygen made up only 1-1½% of the earth's atmosphere (vs. 21% in today's atmosphere). If asphyxiation didn't kill us, lethal ultraviolet rays would, because the low concentration of oxygen (O_2) meant that there was miniscule production of ozone (O_3)—the high-altitude molecule that today saves us from lethal radiation doses. The low-lying, primitive North American continent, somewhat smaller than today's land mass, had its western shore just east of the Tuolumne

Meadows area. Actually, this continent back then was only a western portion of a supercontinent called Pangaea. If we explored this supercontinent, we would find it lifeless due to the excessive radiation—a condition our present world might be plunged into if enough high-flying SSTs are allowed to fly and, as some reputable scientists think, destroy our protective ozone layer. Over this lifeless land mass and its adjacent Sierran sea, the sun set 410 times a year, the days being 2½ hours shorter because the earth rotated faster back then.

Throughout the Silurian period, primitive plants continued building up the earth's supply of oxygen, thereby also increasing ozone production. Given increased protection from ultraviolet rays, life was now capable of existing at or close to the ocean's surface, and coral reefs now formed where environmental conditions were suitable. By the start of the Devonian period, about 400 million years ago, oxygen and ozone existed in sufficient quantities to allow life to move ashore, and soon great forests of primitive tropical trees covered much of the land. In the *Tuolumne Meadows* quad, however, the "land" still consisted of marine sediments lying beneath a warm, shallow sea—although a chain of volcanic islands, similar to today's Japanese Islands, might have existed just west of this area. Since life was now capable of living in all levels and habitats of the sea, it evolved into a complex array of species, with fish becoming very abundant and dominant in this geologic period.

Not until the Devonian period gave way to the Carboniferous period, about 350 million years ago, was our area lifted above the ocean surface for the first time, as the western edge of the supercontinent Pangaea underwent an *orogeny*—a mountain-building episode. Over several tens of millions of years, our area's marine sediments were slowly thrust eastward by large, global forces, resulting in a low range of fold mountains similar to today's Appalachian range. Not only was the landscape changed, but also the rocks composing it. Marine sediments such as shale and other rocks were exposed to intense pressure and high temperatures, transforming them into slate and other metamorphic rocks. In the *Tuolumne Meadows* quad, remnants of these and younger metamorphic rocks are mostly confined to the quad's northeast corner, generally east of the Sierra crest. Near Ireland Lake, however, is a good-sized exposure of metamorphic rocks, and near May Lake and Glen Aulin are small exposures.

Because our quad back then was located very close to the equator, it had a hot, humid climate, which was capable of eroding down the low mountains about as fast as they were being lifted up. A green mantle of dense forest covered this landscape, and in its humid confines thrived a dazzling array of amphibians, large and small, the smaller ones preying on the overabundant insects and other arthropods while trying to avoid becoming the prey of their larger relatives.

The Carboniferous period gave way to the Permian—last of the Paleozoic periods—and amphibians gave way to reptiles as the dominant animal form. Throughout most of the Permian period the *Tuolumne Meadows* quad, like most of the Sierra, was not geologically active, and it was eroded to a fairly low, gentle landscape, then finally overridden by the encroaching sea. However, toward the end of the Permian period a second orogeny began. This time explosive volcanic eruptions covered the shallow sea floor and adjacent land mass with layers of *rhyodacite* ash flows, which had a composition very similar to the volcanic rocks that today compose Lassen Peak in northern California. This orogeny, which began about 230 million years ago, was probably brought about by the incipient break-up of Pangaea.

To understand this breakup and the ensuing geologic events, we must first talk about *plates*. The earth's crust is composed of large, rigid, moving plates, and similar plates have probably existed for at least 4 billion years. Continents, being composed of light-density rocks, are embedded in the tops of these plates. Pangaea, locked onto a giant plate, began to break up when this plate began to break up. Viewed in simplified terms, two plates began to pull away from a newly formed north-south cleft that soon widened to become the embryonic North Atlantic Ocean. As the plates drifted apart—at the rate of about one inch per year—molten lava from below solidified along each plate's trailing edge, so that a big gash in the earth's surface never developed. Today, Iceland sits atop this zone, where separation is still going on. As the North American continent was taken for a piggyback ride west atop a giant plate, this plate's leading edge was overriding another plate that was heading east, forcing the latter plate's edge down into the earth's *mantle*. As this diving edge descended to depths of 100 miles or more, it underwent partial melting, which created intermediate-density molten masses called *magmas*. These high-temperature magmas slowly worked their way up into the lower crust—the floor of the continental rocks such as the ancient marine sediments—and caused these silica-rich rocks to melt and form granitic magmas. It was these granitic magmas that reached the surface in the late Permian period and produced the rhyodacite ash flows. (Rhyolite and dacite are eruptive forms of granite.)

Upward movement of any magma is an extremely slow process, requiring perhaps 5-10 million years, and consequently many granitic magmas never reached the surface. Rather, they solidified as *plutons*, usually 3-5 miles below it. A belt of these plutons, lying just east of today's Sierra crest, became emplaced in the earth's crust over a time span from 210 to 195 million years ago. None of the resulting granitic rocks can be found in the *Tuolumne Meadows* quad, but they are found mostly to the east of it, particularly in Lee Vining canyon. During the following periods, the Jurassic and Cretaceous, four more belts of granitic plutons were emplaced, the youngest being about 80 million years old. These young plutons are the ones that are seen throughout most of the quad today. However, near the quad's west edge, in the Mt. Hoffmann area, is an intermediate-age belt of plutons.

What was the *Tuolumne Meadows* landscape like during the Mesozoic era, the time when these five belts of plutons were emplaced? It seems that, generally speaking, each belt was formed roughly 20 million years after an orogeny. The first of these orogenies, coinciding with the initial breakup of Pangaea about 230 million years ago, probably produced a tropical-vegetated, low-mountain landscape similar to that of the Devonian orogeny, mentioned earlier. Weathering and erosion then greatly planed down this landscape before the start of the next mountain-building episode. Throughout the Mesozoic era, North America was drifting north as well as west, and as the Yosemite area entered more temperate latitudes, the erosive forces within it probably diminished, yet a high range never formed. During each episode when granite was being intruded in the Sierra Nevada, a vast shallow sea developed to the east of it, flooding most of our southwestern states.

Although mammals and dinosaurs both evolved during the early Mesozoic, it was the dinosaurs who established absolute command, reigning unchallenged for 150 million years over the Mesozoic landscape. Long thought to be cold-blooded, slow and dull, they are now known to have been warm-blooded, many were extremely fast, and some were quite intelligent. Large body size helped maintain their body temperature. The smaller flying reptiles were also warm-blooded, preserving body heat through insulation by hair or hairlike feathers. During the Cretaceous period a large sea existed where the Coast Ranges stand today, and near its shore roamed duck-billed hadrosaurs while strong-limbed mosasaurs and plesiosaurs—common in most children's dinosaur books—prowled the sea. Dinosaurs didn't entirely disappear without descendants; rather, by the end of this period they had given rise to a great variety of birds.

As the Mesozoic era yielded to the Cenozoic era, about 65 million years ago, the northern hemisphere's climate cooled dramatically, perhaps due in large part to the contemporaneous opening of the extreme North Atlantic and the Arctic Ocean. Dinosaurs and several marine-life forms disappeared equally dramatically. The conifer group, in existence for 200 million years, now was dominated by pines rather than red-woods, and, joined by flowering plants—in existence for only 50 million years—they clothed the land with an array of plant species not too different from today's. Mammals, however, now beginning to fill ecological niches vacated by recently extinct dinosaurs, looked very different by today's standards. Furthermore, their Sierran landscape was low, for the Sierra Nevada had been appreciably worn down.

During the Eocene epoch, about 55 to 36 million years ago, the Sierra experienced a partial return to a wet, warm climate, which helped to create intense weathering, but then the climate began a long, cooling, drying trend. By mid-Oligocene times, about 30 million years ago, most of the old metamorphic rocks above the granite had been eroded away, transforming the landscape into a largely granitic terrain whose highest summits rose only several thousand feet above sea level. The area of Tuolumne Meadows itself probably stood at about 1000 feet elevation. By now, small and infrequent volcanic outbursts showered the landscape with patches of rhyolite, and they continued well into the Miocene epoch. Then, about 20 million years ago, floods of volcanic flows and water-saturated volcanic mudflows—both chiefly *andesite* in composition—began to inundate much of the topography. Buried in these extensive deposits were remnants of Sierran trees, which back then were oak, elm, beech, walnut, persimmon and avocado.

Extensive vulcanism continued through the first half of the Pliocene epoch, about 6 or 7 million years ago, and then it stopped. Virtually all the eruptions had occurred northeast of the *Tuolumne Meadows* quad, with subsequent flows entering the quad's then-shallow canyons. During this extended period of vulcanism, only one eruption occurred *within* the quad, namely, at Little Devils Postpile, near Glen Aulin, which erupted about 9.4 million years ago. At the time of that eruption the land east of the present-day Sierra crest had been slowly rising along with the Sierra, a process that had been going on since around the start of the Pliocene, about 12 million years

Little Devils Postpile

ago. But beginning about 9 million years ago, and in particular between 7 and 3 million years ago, the land to the east of the present Sierra dropped about a mile in relation to the rising Sierra. During this period, the Sierra's increasing height meant cooler temperatures and more precipitation. Then less moisture was left in the ocean-born storms which reached the Great Basin area, east of the Sierra. As the Great Basin lands became drier, giant sequoias, which had previously thrived there, faced extinction. Some of these big trees migrated over the Sierra passes, such as our area's Tioga Pass, about 4 or 5 million years ago.

At the close of the Pliocene epoch, 3 million years ago, Mts. Conness, Dana and Lyell stood close to 10,000 feet high, and on their north slopes some of the Sierra's first glaciers formed. During the next 3 million years as many as 50 or more glaciers would wax and wane on these and other mountain slopes as the *Tuolumne Meadows* quad rose another 3000 feet. In dozens of episodes the glaciers extended down-canyon for miles, creating the deep, wide, unmistakably glaciated canyons we see today. During the last 85,000 years—the Wisconsin period of the Pleistocene ("Ice Age") epoch—glaciers advanced down the quad's canyons three times. Although each advance typically lasted 20,000 years and the glaciers were often 500-1000 feet thick, only a few feet of the resistant granitic rock floors would be eroded away with each episode.

Asian man appeared on the scene by the time of the last glacial retreat, which took place between 12,000 and 10,000 years ago. Other Asian migrants certainly came to America earlier, but they had little effect on the landscape. The latest migrants, however, were effective big-game hunters, and in 3500 years they excelled at overkill and drove into extinction many large species, including the mastodon, the giant beaver, the long-horned bison, the dire wolf and the saber-toothed cat. In other continents man was carrying out similar extermination campaigns. Big game, however, was never abundant in our area, for the *Tuolumne Meadows* quad quickly became forested after each glaciation.

Our landscape received its final touch in the last 2500 years, during which several small ice ages occurred. The Sierran glaciers we see today are remnants of the last of these. It was during these wet times that Tuolumne Meadows and many other High Sierra meadows formed—due to rises in groundwater tables which killed off the trees. We can be thankful for this event, for without the meadows, the rugged peaks of our spectacular landscape would certainly be less photogenic.

The Fauna

Black Bears and Backpackers

By far the most discussed animal in Tuolumne Meadows is the black bear (*Ursus americanus*). Indeed, even entering the Park you are exposed to bear literature and signs that warn you of possible confrontation with this magnificent, highly intelligent carnivore. That it is the largest carnivore in the Park, often exceeding 400 pounds, brings nightmares to some novice hikers in Yosemite. An unplanned, face-to-face, late-night awakening by one of these furry fellows is sure to stir up the adrenalin. But though a carnivore by structure, the black bear is largely a herbivore by habit. The diet of Yosemite bears is about 85-95% vegetable matter, and most of their animal intake is in the form of insects, occasionally fish or fawns, but never people. With their long tongues they busily lick up all the scurrying ants, buzzing hornets and other hapless invertebrates that their powerful paws expose in a rotting log. Throughout the entire history of Yosemite National Park, not even one visitor has lost his life to one of these *usually* gentle beasts. That they could easily harm us if they wanted to is an understatement—anyone who has witnessed one of these fellows peeling open the door of a small car can testify to the bear's superhuman strength.

To the average Yosemite black bear, your car is a veritable cornucopia of culinary delights. VW owners are particularly susceptible. In days past, many a hiker parked his VW at a trailhead or in a campground. The bears, in time, learned how to open this "canned food," and today every well-educated Yosemite bear can perform this feat, among others, in his vast repertoire of gustatory pursuits. Today, other small foreign cars, particularly hatchbacks, are opened almost as easily. In contrast, large American cars, due to their heavier frames and trunks, provide the bears with problems. But *no* car's food is

safe if the bear decides to break a window, which he can easily
do. Therefore, keep your food locked in the trunk, keep the
car's interior *empty,* and hope for the best. *Any* box or bag in
the back seat may stimulate brother bruin's salivary glands.
Needless to say, anyone leaving a convertible unattended is
inviting an easy—and costly—"rip-off!"

It is one thing to have your car's window broken, but it is a
more serious matter to have your food stolen when you are
three days out from your trailhead on your one-week backpacking vacation. To avoid hunger pangs, first thoroughly read
the bear literature the rangers hand out at the Park's entrances.
In the past, hikers thought they were safe when they hung
their food over a stout limb, with the food far from the tree
trunk, and tied their end of the rope around the trunk. But
some of them found out bears can gnaw through the rope or
rip through it with their claws. Now the more popular backcountry campsites have steel cables strung between trees.
Using the counterbalance system, you can suspend your bag of
food over the cable, counterbalanced at the other end of your
short rope by another weight—a rock or perhaps a second food
bag (see photo). The bags should be at least 12 feet off the
ground, not 10 feet as earlier thought, for, contrary to popular
opinion, some large bears will leap up to reach your suspended
food. Thoughtful hikers leave poles around with which you
can push your food bag up out of the bear's reach once you've
got the other end of the rope over the cable and weighted.
Thoughtless hikers chop up these poles for firewood. Where
food cables don't exist, you'll have to try counterbalancing
your food over a tree limb. Picking the right-sized slightly
downcurving limb takes experience, for it must be too small
for a bear or even a bear cub to climb out on, yet large enough
so the bear won't break it off. And of course your food should
be out of a climbing bear's grasp, well away from the tree
trunk. Although black bears, as opposed to grizzly bears, are
adept tree climbers, they are poor rock climbers, so you might
look for a nearby small cliff ledge to store your food on.

Avoiding *popular* campsites increases your chances of having a bear-free, restful night. But don't think that because you set up camp above timberline—the bear's *usual* upper limit—you're surely out of bear country. Even if you camp at rocky, alpine Donohue Pass, you may still meet Mr. Bear. Passes, especially those with trails, are used by black bears in their travels, which may cover 60 miles or more. Indeed, tagged Yosemite bears have shown up at the wrong end of hunters' guns in the Lake Tahoe area, about 150 trail miles north of Tuolumne Meadows. This emigration is one of the ways Yosemite's bear population is kept in check.

Counterbalanced bearbagging

Numbering about 320 individuals, Yosemite's bear population is greater than the area's natural carrying capacity, for many bears rely in part on food procured at campgrounds, trailheads and campsites. Until the late 1960s they also relied on garbage dumps, and when these were banned, they concentrated their efforts on trash bins. These were bearproofed in 1974, leaving bears with only their natural food sources and the visitors' unattended supplies. If humans were banned from Yosemite, many bears would go hungry. Lucky for us, the National Park Service does not plan to keep us out of this alpine wonderland. Fortunately for the black bears, they will not starve.

Birth control—still a dirty word to some people—insures that the black bears won't outgrow their food supply. Briefly during summer, the female bear tolerates the presence of a male in order to mate. However, the blastula—an early embryo stage—does not implant in the female's uterus until November, just before she retires to her den for the winter. If the female's food supply has been low, the blastula she carries will fail to implant and will self-abort. However, if her food has been sufficient, the blastula will implant and grow, becoming, in mid-winter, a newborn, tiny half-pound cub. The female usually gives birth to her first young when she reaches three years of age. Usually her first litter consists of a single cub, with whom she emerges in late spring's retreating snows and whom she nurses, protects and instructs through the summer. Soon after both arouse from their next winter's sleep—a form of hibernation—the female chases the yearling away so that in summer she may again be receptive to a male to again begin this reproductive two-year cycle. With the second and following litters, two cubs will usually be born, although litters of one, three and four are not uncommon. Although we call these bears "black bears," they can be black, brown, buff or cinnamon, and cubs of the same litter may be different colors.

On his own, the yearling is probably facing the most traumatic time of his life—foraging for himself. If he is capable of storing up enough fat on his own to survive the oncoming winter, he will have earned his adulthood, and very likely he will live to a ripe old age (12-15+ years in the wild). Hopefully, his mother taught him well, thus allowing us, under the proper circumstances, to enjoy the sight of this patient, intelligent mammalian cousin. What the female teaches her cubs in part depends on our behavior. If we don't provide her with the temptations of our food, she won't be as willing to teach her young to rely upon it, and in the end, both backpacker and black bear will be better off.

Belding Ground Squirrels

Common as bears are, they are far outnumbered in Tuolumne Meadows by Belding ground squirrels. This squirrel is found on almost all Sierran meadows, and his alert and inquisitive stance, coupled with his cheerful whistle, is a friendly accompaniment to meadow-walking.

When he wants to have a look around, he stands up very straight and still on his hind legs, with his forelegs against his body, and from any distance he looks like a small stake or picket pin. In fact, some people call him a "picket pin."

Belding ground squirrel

The Belding is smaller than a California ground squirrel—about 10 inches long including his short tail. He doesn't climb trees, and seldom even climbs on rocks; to spy out enemies, he merely stands tall. When he sees an intruder, he makes a piercing whistle to warn his colony, and zips into his meadow hole—or even into your tent. He can be seen begging handouts at Tuolumne Meadows Lodge, and will help himself to your food if you give him a chance. Don't. In the long run, your food will do him more harm than good.

Trout

As recently as a few years ago, about 160 of the Park's lakes were stocked with rainbow and brook trout, and, to a lesser extent, with brown, golden and cutthroat trout. The Park is now trying to return these lakes (and also streams) to a more natural, precivilized condition, and consequently about 1/3 of these lakes will be allowed to go barren. Limited stocking will continue at popular lakes.

As one might expect, lakes close to Highway 120 and lakes along popular trails attract the most fishermen, so you might do better to select a more remote lake or stream to fish in. However, avoid lakes at the higher elevations, for they tend to be barren or to have only undersized trout. In the past we and others (including the National Park Service) have dispensed information on fishing pressure at various lakes. The result was that many fishermen flocked to sites said to have light fishing pressure, thereby radically changing the situation and playing havoc with planning the fish-planting schedule. In this edition we'll let you select your own fishing sites; there are still plenty around. Be sure you have your fishing license, which can be obtained at the Tuolumne Meadows Store and at other localities.

"Agesilaus being invited once to hear a man who admirably imitated the nightingale, he declined, saying he had heard the nightingale itself."   Plutarch

The Flora

DESPITE ITS OBVIOUS ALPINE character, most of the *Tuolumne Meadows* quadrangle is forested, and the tree that unquestionably dominates its forests is the lodgepole pine. Thin-barked, sappy and perhaps least impressive of the High Sierra conifers, this pine forms dense stands that shade the winter's snowfall, thereby preserving snow patches well into the summer. Pure, dense stands, however, invite attack, and lodgepoles have suffered heavy casualties from lodgepole needleminers—small moths whose sheer numbers of larvae and pupae devour the trees' needles. Witness the ghost forest of lodgepole snags alongside Highway 120 between Polly Dome and Fairview Dome.

Lodgepoles also face attack in the form of competition from other species. On shady, north-facing slopes, where temperatures are cooler and snow lingers longer, mountain hemlocks grow and sometimes dominate over the lodgepoles. These two trees, because they are adapted to moist-soil conditions, are both indicators of abundant mosquito populations, and as any veteran Yosemite hiker knows, the *Tuolumne Meadows* quad seems to have more than its share of mosquitoes. The meadows themselves are nearly unbearable in early summer, when the water table (the level below which the ground is completely saturated with water) is at or just below the surface.

It is a high water table that prevents lodgepoles from *successfully* invading Tuolumne Meadows and other subalpine meadows, or drives them out if they are there. With the onset of one or more stages of the Little Ice Age, which we are still in, the water table in the Tuolumne Meadows area rose and this overall rise killed the lodgepoles, thus bringing the meadows into existence about either 2500 or 1200 years ago. Sedges in particular thrive in moist environments, and they are by far the main type of vegetation seen in the meadows today. These "grasses" together with meadow wildflowers, bushes and true grasses can change their physiology to cope with early-season water-saturated soils. Through evapotranspiration

Lodgepole pines

(plant water loss to atmosphere), these plants significantly lower the meadow's water table by the end of summer. If they become too effective, of course, they invite an invasion by lodgepoles.

Reflecting again on lodgepoles, the observant hiker will note that this pine competes with more plants than just hemlocks, sedges, grasses and meadow flowers. On well-drained slopes that receive a lot of precipitation, red firs and/or silver pines may locally dominate the terrain. On drier slopes, particularly south-facing ones, Jeffrey pines spread their limbs, creating a more open, often aromatic forest. Where large granite exposures interrupt the lodgepole forest, western junipers exploit the sparse soil that develops in the granite cracks. At lower elevations, with their warmer temperatures, lodgepoles lose out to sugar pines just as red firs lose out to white firs. At the other end of the elevation spectrum, lodgepoles give way to whitebark pines, which thrive near and at timberline. Whitebarks, unlike lodgepoles, can greatly modify their size and shape to suit the harsh timberline environment. Near mountain passes, where icy winter winds would freeze any exposed living matter, this tree grows as a dense, waist-high bush. In such a reduced state, it waits out the cruel winter, its needles protected by an insulating cover of snow.

Alpine wildflowers too must adapt to a subfreezing winter environment, which for them can be 10 or 11 months out of the year. For annuals, it is important that they grow very fast to produce seeds before the icy temperatures of September kill them off. Perennials, on the other hand, can afford to grow at a more relaxed pace, and they store up food supplies to sustain them till the next growing season. Among the most successful alpine perennials are a group of plant species known as cushion plants. Typically ½ inch high or less, these domelike plants resemble pincushions in shape and feel, their dense foliage giving them a spongy texture. Being low to the ground, they avoid virtually all the wind, thereby reducing water loss. Their dome shape, which presents a minimum of surface exposure for a given volume, further reduces water loss. Dead leaves stay in place, thereby enriching the density of the cushion plant. This has several benefits. The dead vegetable matter absorbs and holds water from summer thunderstorms, it traps dust particles—which also can hold water—and the vegetable matter decays in place, thus recycling nutrients back to the plant.

All alpine plants are dwarf, so that their flowers, which are normal-sized, appear large. When the flowers are not blooming, the alpine environment may appear desolate and barren. In reality, this environment is a complex of microenvironments, and each has its devoted assemblage of plant species. To appreciate the complexity of such an assemblage, or the marvelous adaptations of a particular species, one must get down on his knees, if not his belly. One of the few conspicuous alpine plants, when in bloom, is the sky pilot, a woody perennial that in midsummer briefly produces a beautiful dense ball of light-blue flowers. This plant seeks the most extreme of microenvironments, the rocky, windswept slopes on the highest peaks.

The best place to reap a bonanza in alpine-wildflower finds is in the quad's northeast corner, which is dominated by metamorphic rocks. For alpine plants, these rocks are definitely advantageous over granitic rocks. Metamorphic rocks fracture into smaller pieces, which form a finer-grained soil, which in turn holds more water than granitic soil does. The soil is darker in color than granitic soil, so it absorbs more heat and thus prolongs the plant's growing period. Finally, the soil is richer in dark minerals, and these are the minerals that provide plant nutrients. When you go botanizing, take along Weeden's *A Survival Handbook to Sierra Flora*. We've field-tested it against all other Sierran flower guides and have found it definitely superior. It is much more than a book on edible plants—it is an accurate, comprehensive, illustrated, *intelligible* flora to the Sierra's ferns, flowers, shrubs and trees.

The Climate

MAN, LIKE THE REST OF the plants and animals with which he shares the land, depends upon the climate. Of particular interest to visitors to Yosemite are the rain forecasts. These forecasts are posted at the Visitor Center in Tuolumne Meadows. Since most backcountry travelers make their treks during the summer months, there is less concern with the winter's precipitation, but as experienced mountaineers already know, the previous winter's snow accumulation can affect both the summer's precipitation rate and the temperatures (not to mention the accessibility of the high country). Large snow packs can "delay" the arrival of spring, and can make many summer nights very cold indeed.

Generally, however, Tuolumne Meadows summers are remarkably dry. When rain does fall during the summer months, it is more likely to take the form of afternoon showers that are preceded and followed by thunderstorms, but even the most optimistic backcountry hiker carries a plastic tarp or the like as insurance.

For the most part, the summertime temperatures of our quadrangle are quite comfortable, but the difference between those around the meadows and, say, Ireland Lake can be as much as 20 degrees. One can usually count on summer maximum temperatures in the lower elevations of the quad of about $70°$ and in the higher elevations of $55-60°$. At night, it often drops below $40°$ in Tuolumne Meadows, and it sometimes freezes even in July and August.

There is a flaw in citing mountain temperatures by the thermometer: the human body responds to wind by getting colder. Incredible as it seems, if the air temperature is $70°$ and the wind velocity is 20 miles per hour, the effective temperature is $30°$. In other words, under these conditions a naked person would be as cold as he would be if standing in still air at $30°$. Our advice: take several layers of clothes that you can add on as the weather gets progressively colder.

Lightning during the quick summer thunderstorms is a danger to be reckoned with, and visitors to the Park should familiarize themselves with the basic lightning facts: 1) When lightning is discharging, avoid being "conspicuous": stay clear of open expanses of water; keep off open expanses of rock or meadow; and stay away from stand-uppish landmarks such as lone, isolated trees. 2) Seek shelter and stay put until the storm is well past. An automobile is a safe place from which to watch a storm's progress. If you are in the backcountry, seek out shelter in dense tree stands that have no particularly outstanding trees. In such an area it is best if you and your friends do *not* huddle together. Also, take off any metal objects you are carrying.

But to precede the traveler's visit to Tuolumne Meadows with dire warnings and a list of "do's and don'ts" is to destroy that prized and terribly fragile element of the wilderness experience called *discovery*. We go to wilderness to discover what is there to be seen and felt; we abandon our defenses against the machines that we left back in Gross National Productland, and listen to the silence. In a few days, we get an inkling of what things matter.

> "I take very seriously the task of awakening, in as many people as possible, a deeper understanding of the awe-inspiring wonder of nature and I am fanatically eager to gain proselytes."
> Konrad Lorenz

The Camps

THE YOSEMITE PARK AND Curry Company runs five "permanent" summer High Sierra camps. Arranged roughly in a circle, they are all in *Tuolumne Meadows* quadrangle except the camp at Merced Lake, which is only a short distance south of our quad.

On the average, these camps are located about nine miles apart (see map in back). They provide accommodations in tents, in which there are beds with springs and mattress, linen, and ample blankets for the cold nights. Breakfast and dinner are served in a central dining tent, and though the fare is simple, it is copious. Each camp has hot showers, which to some hikers are even more thrilling than not having to make camp and cook dinner.

These camps are partially dismantled in the fall and re-erected as soon as snow conditions allow in early summer, and each camp therefore opens at a slightly different time. In most years all the camps are open by mid-July and remain open through the Labor Day weekend.

Glen Aulin Camp (7850′), on the Tuolumne River, is centrally located along this river's stretch of beautiful, fantastic cascades and waterfalls.

Sunrise Camp (9350′) is on a long, rather narrow shelf a few feet above Long Meadow. It boasts inspiring morning and evening views across the meadow to magnificent peaks.

May Lake Camp (9320′) lies beneath the eastern wall of Mt. Hoffman, on the shore of May Lake. Of all the camps, it is closest to a road.

Merced Lake Camp (7230′) stands in a dense forest near the east shore of Merced Lake. Lowest of the camps, this one is the most likely to have fairly warm swimming, and probably has the best fishing.

Vogelsang Camp (10,180′) is the highest camp, and the most dramatically situated. Near timberline, it provides easy access to alpine lakes, slopes and meadows.

Tuolumne Meadows Lodge (8720′) is a lodge you can drive to. Accommodations here consist of tent tops on wooden platforms, each with plain beds and a table plus a wood stove for warmth. You cannot cook in a tent. Breakfast and dinner are served in the canvas-topped restaurant close beside the rollicking Dana Fork of the Tuolumne River. You pay for meals separately from accommodations, and one can eat there without sleeping there.

You can do the whole loop of camps by yourself on your own schedule, or you can sign up for a seven-day hiking trip guided by a ranger-naturalist of the Park Service, who explains what you are seeing.

Reservations at the camps are becoming increasingly hard to get, so write at the very beginning of January if you wish to be sure. Prices are not cheap, but for no more than the price of a motel you can avoid having to carry very much and enjoy a large dinner and breakfast, to say nothing of that hot shower. The address for camp and trip reservations for the High Sierra camps and the Lodge is: Reservations, Yosemite Park & Curry Co., Yosemite National Park CA 95389. You can also call toll-free from anywhere in California: (800) 692-5811 or 372-4671.

Vogelsang camp

The Trails

IN THIS AGE OF MAN AS THE Great Spectator, there is an urgent need for physical involvement and commitment. The glass and steel of the modern-day automobile stand between man and the land, and if any real perspective is to be acquired in this country, man must emerge from his mechanical cocoon and walk the trails. The *Tuolumne Meadows* quadrangle offers a variety of hikes that will suit both young and old, both very active and less active people. The trail descriptions that follow are divided into three categories: 1) **day hikes**, 2) **main trails** and 3) **lateral trails**, which link main trails or extend day hikes. A few cross-country routes are also described briefly.

The day hikes range in exertion from leisurely to moderate. A spirited hiker in good condition could round-trip many of the main trails in a day—but why bother? Anyone in fair condition can make it from one High Sierra Camp to the next in a day, since he doesn't have to carry food and bedding on his back—if he has made reservations months in advance (see the chapter "The Camps" and Main Trail #9).

THE TRAILHEADS

The locations of the 14 trailheads listed below are given by their map coordinates, such as "C3".

1. **May Lake Trailhead**: 1.7 miles from the Tioga Road at a signed turnoff 3.7 miles west of the Tenaya Lake Walk-in Campground. A4.

2. **Tenaya Lake Walk-in Campground**: At the southwest end of Tenaya Lake. A4.

3. **Murphy Creek Trailhead**: Across from a picnic area midway along Tenaya Lake 0.6 mile northeast of the walk-in campground. A4.

4. **Budd Creek Trailhead**: 1.5 miles west of the store and post office and .7 mile east of Pothole Dome. C3.

5. **Elizabeth Lake Trailhead**: At the southeast end of Tuolumne Meadows Campground. Walk up to the Group Camping

Section and find the trail across from a masonry building. C3.

6. **Lyell Fork Trailhead**: Beside the Lyell Fork at the east end of Tuolumne Meadows Campground. D3.

7. **Dog Lake Trailhead**: 0.1 mile west of the Tioga Road, turning off just east of the bridge over the Tuolumne River. C3.

8. **Soda Springs**: 0.3 mile west of the Tioga Road, turning off just east of the bridge over the Tuolumne River. C3.

9. **Lembert Dome Trailhead**: The midway lot—see next entry. D3.

10. **Tuolumne Meadows Lodge**: Along the south side of the Lodge's parking lot at the end of a blacktop spur road that leaves the Tioga Road 0.5 mile east of the bridge over the Tuolumne River. You can park here only if you are a Lodge guest. Others must park in the parking lot near the west end of this spur road or the lot midway along this spur road. D3.

11. **Mono Pass Trailhead**: 5.6 miles east of the Visitor Center, or 1.4 miles south of Tioga Pass. E3.

12. **Tioga Pass**: Yosemite National Park boundary, 7.0 miles northeast of the Visitor Center. E2.

13. **Gardisky Lake Trailhead**: 2.1 miles north on Highway 120 from Tioga Pass, then 1.1 miles northeast toward Saddlebag Lake. E1.

14. **Saddlebag Lake**: 1.3 miles northwest past the Gardisky Lake Trailhead. E1.

> "Within these plantations of God a decorum and sanctity reign, a perennial festival is dressed, and the guest sees not how he should tire of them in a thousand years. In the woods we return to reason and faith."
>
> Ralph Waldo Emerson

Trail Descriptions

(The map coordinates of the start of a trail appear after its mileage in the heading for the trail.)

DAY HIKE #1

May Lake

1.2 miles, or 2.0 km, one way (A4)

Although this walk is treated here as a day hike, there is no reason, really, save inability to make a reservation, that one should not stay overnight at the May Lake High Sierra Camp. If you don't have reservations, you can camp out in the hikers' camp just above the lake's south shore.

The trail begins by a small pond on Snow Flat in a moderately dense stand of hemlock, red fir, and silver and lodgepole pine. Visible in the northwest is the peak which is at the geographic center of the Park, Mt. Hoffmann. In a little vale to the east of the trail, water lies late in the season, permitting corn lilies to bloom into August. Our sandy trail ascends gently through mixed forest cover, where we recognize the silver pine by its long, narrow cones and checkerboard bark pattern, and we notice how the red-fir cones, near the tops of these trees, stand upright on the branches, unlike the hanging cones of pines and spruces.

The initial ascent leads up open granite slabs dotted with lodgepoles. Then, as we switchback west up a short, steep slope, we have fine views of Cathedral Peak in the east, Mt. Clark in the southeast, and Half Dome and Clouds Rest in the south. Near the top of the slope, the forest cover thickens and the silver pines become larger and handsomer. Just beyond the crest, we find ourselves in a duff-covered flat beneath half a dozen superb large hemlock trees, and we are at deep-blue May Lake. Swimming is not allowed, but you may try your luck at catching the lake's brook trout or rainbow trout while contemplating the lake's beautiful backdrop of the east slopes of massive Mt. Hoffmann. The steep but safe, popular and easy climb to its summit is described in the next hike.

May Lake

DAY HIKE #2

Mt. Hoffmann

3.0 miles, or 4.9 km, one way (A4)

Mt. Hoffmann, centrally located in Yosemite National Park, provides the best all-around views of this park's varied landscapes. Perhaps more hikers ascend it than any other high peak

Pinnacle on Mt. Hoffmann

in the Park, with only Mt. Lyell and Mt. Dana challenging its popularity. As with any 2-mile-high peak ascent, wear dark glasses, for there's 1/3 less air on the summit, and the ultra-violet rays come on strong. Also, avoid altitude sickness, which is brought on by overexerting yourself, particularly after a large breakfast. Take it easy, for the route is short. However, abandon your attempt—as on *any* peak—if a thunderstorm is approaching.

Follow Day Hike #1 to May Lake, above whose southeast corner you'll see a trail striking west. This immediately passes the camping area, then traverses across metamorphic rocks cropping out above the lake's southwest shore. You now follow it south, first through a small gap, then through a boulder-strewn wildflower garden. You might lose the trail here, but the route south—up a shallow gully to a small, linear meadow—is quite obvious.

From the meadow's south end, near a saddle, the trail goes 100 yards southwest, leaves the quadrangle, and climbs north-west up to the broad, lupine-decked summit plateau. Unsuspecting hikers often end up going several hundred yards past the meadow, following misleading ducks.

Numerous summits exist; all should be visited. The western summit is the highest, and you have an easy, safe scramble to its top. Having lunch here, you'll almost certainly attract marmots, begging a meal. Please don't feed them. If you've brought along a map of the park, you should be able to identify almost every major peak in or bordering it, since most are visible from here. Note how Mt. Hoffmann's nearly flat summit plateau contrasts with the mountain's steep sides. Glaciers have eaten back into all sides of this mountain, almost destroying this plateau, which like those on Mt. Conness, Dana Plateau, Dore Pass, and a few other spots was once part of an extensive, rolling landscape that existed as much as 50 million years ago. When you return, take the beaten path you ascended. Other routes are steeper, have loose rock and are potentially dangerous.

DAY HIKE #3

Clouds Rest

7.0 miles, or 11.2 km, one way (A3)

Although Clouds Rest is higher than Half Dome, it is easier and safer to climb, and it provides far better views of the park than does popular, sometimes overcrowded Half Dome. But it is 14 miles round trip. Except for its last 300 yards, the Clouds Rest Trail lacks the terrifying, potentially lethal drop-offs found along Half Dome's shoulder and back side, thereby making it a good trail for acrophobic photographers.

Follow Main Trail #3 three miles up to the Sunrise Lakes trail junction. Then, with all the hard climbing behind you, descend south along the Forsyth Trail. This switchbacks down to a shady, sometimes damp flat, then climbs up to a block-strewn ridge that sprouts dense clumps of chinquapin and aspen. Beyond it the trail descends briefly to a tree-fringed pond—adequate for camping—then wanders south for ½ mile before veering west to cross three creeklets, which will be your last reliable sources of water. After you cross the first creeklet, follow the trail—sometimes hard to find—briefly downstream, then veer left to cross the second creeklet before climbing up to the third. Beyond it the trail rapidly eases its gradient and soon reaches the Clouds Rest Trail junction.

The Forsyth Trail (Lateral Trail #4) forks left, but we keep right, ascend the Clouds Rest Trail west to a forested, gravelly crest and follow it down to a shallow saddle. Our final ascent begins here. After a moderate ascent of ¼ mile, we emerge from the forest cover to get our first excellent views of Tenaya Canyon and the countryside west and north of it. After another ¼ mile along the crest we come to an easily missed junction with an unseen horse trail. If you're riding a horse from Tenaya Lake to Yosemite Valley via the Clouds Rest Trail—the most scenic of the possible routes to the valley— you'll want to take this hidden trail after walking to the summit. It starts at a fairly large silver pine that is 80 yards past a good view. The Clouds Rest Trail more or less dies out here, so scramble 15 feet up to the narrow crest. Acrophobics may not want to hike any farther, but here they can get some spactacular views of Tenaya Canyon, Half Dome and Yosemite Valley which are nearly identical with those seen from the summit. Spreading below is the expansive 4500-foot-high face of Clouds Rest—the largest granite face in the park.

Those who follow the now steeper, narrow, almost trailless crest 300 yards to the summit are further rewarded with views of the Clark Range and the Merced River Canyon. Growing on the rocky summit are a few knee-high Jeffrey pines and white-bark pines plus assorted bushes and wildflowers. Some hikers like to spend a waterless night on the summit in order to experience the matchless sunrise. If you do this, pack out your litter and make your latrine off the summit—it is too small to withstand pollution. If you plan to continue to Yosemite Valley, you'll rejoin the horse trail in ½ mile, and then in about 3 miles, after descending past some impressive scenery, you'll reach the John Muir Trail (see the *Yosemite* High Sierra Hiking Guide).

Right: View from Clouds Rest

DAY HIKE #4

Polly Dome Lakes

3.1 miles, or 5.0 km, to the largest lake (A4)

Our trail, up seasonally flowing Murphy Creek, climbs three miles north to a junction with the High Sierra Camps Loop Trail (Main Trail #9). We take this uneventful trail most of the way, passing a bridge across Murphy Creek early on our hike. The trail south from it descends to within a few yards of the western of the two Tenaya Lake Walk-in Campgrounds.

Midway along our hike is ample evidence of glacier action: glacier-transported boulders and glacier-polished bedrock slabs. Across these slabs the trail can disappear, so watch for ducks (man-made stone piles). Near the divide at the head of Murphy Creek you'll reach a trailside pond, on your right. Leave the trail here and progress cross-country ½ mile southeast to the north shore of the largest of the Polly Dome Lakes. Any cross-country route you might take will tend to get a little damp and/or brushy, but the distance is short and the lake is almost impossible to miss, particularly since it lies at the base of Polly Dome. The best campsites are along the west shore of this warm, shallow, boulder-dotted lake. The small lakes northeast of it aren't worth your effort unless you happen to like mosquitoes.

"As we advance in life, we acquire a keener sense of the value of time. Nothing else, indeed, seems of any consequence; and we become misers in this respect."

William Hazlitt

Small Polly Dome Lake

Largest Polly Dome Lake

Cathedral Peak and Lower Cathedral Lake

DAY HIKE #5

Lower Cathedral Lake

3.8 miles, or 6.2 km, one way (C3)

This very popular hike is often done as an overnighter. Morning and evening rays upon Cathedral Peak, just east of the lake, provide the hiker with the inspiration one would expect from this ice-carved temple of Nature. This hike is described as the first part of Main Trail #1.

DAY HIKE #6

Budd Lake

2.7 miles, or 4.3 km, one way (C3)

The unsigned trail up Budd Creek can be hard to find. From the Budd Creek trailhead walk 90 yards southwest to a junction with the John Muir Trail, then start southwest up it toward the Cathedral Lakes. After a long ¼ mile, you'll come to two lodgepole snags on the south side of the trail, one leaning against the other. On the uphill side of one are an arrow and the words "Budd Lake." The John Muir Trail curves *northwest* here, the only place it does so on this part of its ascent. From the snags at this bend you'll see the faint Budd Creek Trail climbing south. The trail quickly becomes more obvious and its first mile is easy to follow. However, at the end of that mile the trail levels off and forks. The obvious branch makes a brief, gentle descent, but the correct branch forks right and climbs up to a granite bench, then heads south along its brink. In about 1/3 mile it rejoins the lower trail, then momentarily becomes vague just before crossing Budd Creek. On the east bank of Budd Creek is a third trail segment, one that has branched off from the lower trail. From the crossing only one trail climbs a short mile up Budd Creek, crossing it again just before reaching Budd Lake.

Along your ascent of this trail you'll note that Unicorn Peak, to the east, has three summits, not one, as you might assume from the name. Although the peak is mentioned in *The Climber's Guide to the High Sierra*, no mention is made of the better climbing on the long cliff below and northwest of the peak.

At Budd Lake camping is no longer allowed to humans, but perhaps you will find an overly friendly marmot waiting to empty your pack while you're off exploring the area. Budd Lake is perhaps unique in Yosemite in that it contains two geologically recent terminal moraines of the Little Ice Age. (A terminal moraine is an arc-shaped accumulation of boulders and debris that had been deposited by a glacier; it marks the point of the glacier's farthest advance down-canyon.) The moraine that dams Budd Lake probably formed about 2500 years ago, while the one found near the lake's south end probably formed about 1000 years ago, if not 500 years ago.

While you're admiring Cathedral Peak, the Echo Peaks and the Cockscomb, which surround this basin, you might take a close look at the 80-million-year-old granitic rock they are made of. Originally it was classified as true granite, more recently as quartz monzonite, and now—by international standards—as granodiorite. Regardless of its classification, it is easy to identify, for it contains large, blocky crystals of potassium feldspar. Climbers new to the Tuolumne Meadows area quickly discover that these make good holds.

Cathedral Peak granodiorite

DAY HIKE #7

Elizabeth Lake

2.4 miles, or 3.8 km, one way (C3)

The signed trail to Elizabeth Lake begins across a road from a masonry building just before the turnaround in the Group Camping Section of the Tuolumne Meadows Campground. Because it starts at the Group Camping Section, this trail is heavily used. (Beyond Elizabeth Lake, the trail is much less used—see Main Trail #8.)

Only 50 yards from the trailhead our T-blazed trail crosses the Tenaya Lake/Lyell Canyon Trail, and then it continues a steady southward ascent. The shade-giving forest cover along this climb is almost entirely lodgepole pine as the trail crosses several runoff streams that dry up by late summer. More than a mile out, the trail veers near Unicorn Creek, and the music of this dashing, gurgling, cold-water stream makes the climbing easier.

After rising 800 feet, the trail levels off, the stunted lodgepole pines are farther spaced, and the hiker emerges at the foot of a long meadow. Partway through the meadow a short spur trail leads southwest to Elizabeth Lake. Few places in Yosemite give so much for so little effort as this lovely subalpine lake. Backdropped by Unicorn Peak, the lake faces the snow-topped peaks of the Sierra crest north of Tuolumne Meadows. From the east and north sides of the lake, the views across the waters to Unicorn Peak are classic, and one can see why this is a traditional lunch spot for people climbing this glacier-trimmed, knife-edge crest. The glacier-carved lake basin is indeed one of the most beautiful in the Tuolumne Meadows area.

DAY HIKE #8

An excursion through Tuolumne Meadows

5.7 miles, or 9.2 km, for the complete loop (C3)

A good way to get acclimatized to this area's high elevation is to take this almost level loop trip through and around Tuolumne Meadows. You can start the loop at any of a number of points, but we'll start our description at the parking lot at the foot of the meadow's prominent landmark, Lembert Dome. Walk west to where the road turns north up to the Tuolumne Meadows Stable, then continue west on a closed dirt road— part of the John Muir Trail. After a pleasant walk with views south of the western Cathedral Range peaks, you go through a low gap and the road forks. Keep right, then in a few paces leave the road and take a short trail to the rust-stained, iron-rich Soda Springs. Being effervescent, they act like tonic water

Tuolumne Meadows panorama

Soda Springs

and can be added to any powdered drink you may have brought along.

From the springs and the adjacent Parsons Memorial Lodge —once the property of the Sierra Club—head south to the large bridge across the Tuolumne River. Lembert Dome, which looks more like a half dome, is plainly seen from the bridge. The dome's northern half, being laced with vertical fractures, was quarried away by repeated episodes of glaciation. Immediately across the bridge we meet a *de facto* trail from the Tuolumne Meadows Store. Fishermen take it out to here to try their skill. The Park trend nowadays is to restore Yosemite to its pre-civilized condition, and this plan includes the cessation of many fish plantings. Most of the Park's lakes will become fishless, but the Tuolumne River, with adequate gravels for trout eggs, should support a natural population.

Leaving the bridge, the John Muir Trail crosses the open meadow, aiming first at Unicorn Peak, with only its northernmost summit showing, then aiming gradually westward at the Cockscomb, the Echo Peaks and finally, near Highway 120, at Cathedral Peak. We cross the highway and, starting by the east end of a trailer-sewage disposal site built in 1976, walk a few minutes south up into a lodgepole forest to meet an east-west trail. On it we go east through the forest, skirt the south border of large Tuolumne Meadows Campground, and at its east end reach a trail junction above the south bank of the Lyell Fork of the Tuolumne River. Now we parallel the Lyell Fork east ¾ mile to a junction, turn left and cross a small meadow to reach two bridges over the Lyell Fork. Note the north-south fracture pattern of the granite here and how it forces the river, when low, to take a tortuous path. When free of such fractures, or joints, granite is almost immune to erosion and even massive glaciers can only shave away a few inches, at best. Try visiting this spot in the evening, as the day's cumulonimbus clouds start breaking up and then turn a fiery red to match the alpenglow on Mt. Dana and Mt. Gibbs.

Evening on the Lyell Fork

Lembert Dome

A short, winding climb north, followed by an equal descent, brings us to the Dana Fork of the Tuolumne River, only 150 yards past a junction with an east-climbing trail to the Gaylor Lakes (Day Hike #11). Immediately beyond the crossing we meet a short spur trail to the Tuolumne Meadows Lodge. Eschewing it, we parallel the Dana Fork downstream and then hear the fork as it makes a small drop into a clear pool, almost cut in two by a protruding granite finger. At the base of this finger, about eight to ten feet down, is an underwater arch—an extremely rare feature in any kind of rock. If you feel like braving the cold water, 50°F at best, you can dive under and swim through it.

Just beyond the pool we approach the Lodge's road, where a short path climbs a few yards up to it and takes one to the entrance of a large parking lot for backpackers. Now we parallel the paved camp road westward, passing the Tuolumne Meadows Ranger Station and quickly reaching a junction. The main road curves north to the sometimes-noisy highway, but we follow the spur road west, to where it curves into a second large parking lot for backpackers. Our road past the lot becomes a closed dirt road and diminishes to a wide trail by the time we arrive at our loop's end, Highway 120, at Lembert Dome.

DAY HIKE #9

Dog Lake Loop

3.1 miles, or 5.0 km, round trip (D3)

From the parking lot 1/3 mile west of the Tuolumne Meadows Lodge parking lot, we walk briefly east toward the lodge, finding our trail head immediately before a dirt road forks left from the lodge's paved road. A three-minute climb northwest on the trail gets us to a crossing of Highway 120, beyond which we climb more steeply up to a broad, lodgepole-forested saddle. Those climbing Lembert Dome (Day Hike #10) leave the trail here.

Immediately beyond the saddle we reach a trail fork. We'll be returning on the left trail, but for now we take the right one and wander northward on easy terrain, arcing along the east end of a shallow, sedge-filled pond before reaching a trail fork just above the south shore of Dog Lake. We go left, toward the lake's outlet, but we could go right on another trail and make a long loop around Dog Lake. At the lake's east end, this trail temporarily dies out in a wet meadow.

Having gone left, we cross the lake's outlet and from the lake's west shore obtain sometimes-reflected views of Mt. Dana, Mt. Gibbs and Mammoth Peak. A long peninsula extends east into the lake from our shoreline, and on it you can walk—usually in knee-deep water—well out into the middle of this large but shallow lake. Because it is shallow and it also receives no direct snowmelt, it is one of our quadrangle's warmest lakes, suitable for swimming and for just plain relaxing. Camping, however, is prohibited. Like many High Sierra lakes, this one is visited in the summer by spotted sandpipers, who usually nest close to the lake's shore. Among the shore boulders you may find metamorphic ones—rocks that could have got here via glacier transport from their source area, the Gaylor Peak/Tioga Hill area. Today no stream connects this area with

Dog Lake, which lies in a purely granitic watershed.

Leaving Dog Lake at the trail junction just west of its outlet, you descend southwest a few minutes to the Young Lakes Trail, follow it a few more minutes to another trail, branching southeast, and take it. You now cross the outlet creek, then head ½ mile east back to the broad saddle you crossed earlier. On this east traverse, you pass a pond that seasonally has wild onions growing in wet ground near its shore. Rather than traverse east past this point, you can stay on the Young Lakes Trail, a longer route, which descends in deep dust southwest to a parking lot at the foot of Lembert Dome, then cross Highway 120 and follow the John Muir Trail—mostly an abandoned road—back to your starting point.

Dog Lake

DAY HIKE #10

Lembert Dome

1.4 miles, or 2.2 km, one way (D3)

Follow Day Hike #9 up to the broad saddle east of Lembert Dome. Leave the trail and contour westward cross country, staying just below the crest. Dog Dome, with its precipitous north face, is reached in about 1/3 mile and is certainly worth the short climb up to its summit. Like all domes in the *Tuolumne Meadows* quadrangle, this one is domelike in appearance only from a certain angle, and generally un-domelike from most other angles. On this dome you'll see several large boulders left behind by a former Glacier. Like the rock of Dog Dome, they are granitic, but unlike it, they lack the large, blocky feldspar crystals. They originally came from an eastern pluton (body of granitic rock).

Lembert Dome from Soda Springs

Exfoliating summit of Lembert Dome

As you approach the summit of larger Lembert Dome, you'll note that the mountain hemlocks and silver pines have been cropped to bush height by icy winter winds. A short scramble, requiring a little use of your hands, takes you up to the dome's exfoliating summit, one which certainly gives you the best view you can possibly get of Tuolumne Meadows, stretched out below you. Furthermore, most of this quad's peaks stand out for easy identification. To the east are rusty, metamorphic Mt. Dana and Mt. Gibbs and gray, granitic Mammoth Peak. To the south are the peaks of the Cathedral Range, to the west is Fairview Dome, and to the north are the Ragged Peak massif and the Sierra crest at Yosemite's northeast boundary.

DAY HIKE #11

Tuolumne Meadows Lodge to Lower Gaylor Lake

4.6 miles, or 7.3 km, one way (D3)

Because this largely viewless route to the Gaylor Lakes is so inferior to the more scenic, much shorter Tioga Pass route (Day Hike #12), it will be treated superficially. From the Tuolumne Meadows Lodge parking lot, walk a minute or so southwest to the John Muir Trail, which immediately crosses the sometimes roaring Dana Fork of the Tuolumne River on a log. Just up from the fork's bank you'll come to a trail junction. Turn left, and hike two miles east up through a forest that grows on a boulder mantle left by a former glacier. Along your second mile you are usually within earshot and sometimes within sight of the Dana Fork. Eventually you rock-hop or wade across it, immediately reach Highway 120, walk a few yards west on it to a resumption of the trail, then follow it north as it more or less parallels Gaylor Lakes creek.

In a short ¼ mile you'll reach a bend in a road. This road is usually closed, but occasionally it is driven on by horse-owners, who make reservations in advance to camp at road's end, about ¼ mile northeast of us. Near this end the trail resumes and then climbs moderately for 1½ miles before levelling off at the south end of large, open Gaylor Lakes basin. An easy, scenic walk through it leads you to the outlet of shallow lower Gaylor Lake, beyond which the trail rapidly dies out (see Day Hike #12 for description of routes in this basin).

"An urban life saps that calm and stolid strength which is necessary for all great effort and stress, physical or intellectual."
                                                                    Havelock Ellis

DAY HIKE #12

Gaylor Lakes

minimum distance: 5.7 miles, or 9.1 km, semiloop trip (E2)

By the restrooms of the Tioga Pass entrance station a sign informs us that *Camping is not allowed* in the Gaylor Lakes area, which includes the Granite Lakes. As the rocky trail ascends steeply through lodgepole forest, we pass a profusion of flowers in season: single-stemmed senecio, Sierra penstemon, Gray's lovage, daisy, pussytoes, little elephant's head, lupine, monkey flower, Sierra wallflower, columbine and corn lily. Shortly beyond the ½ *mile* sign we come to a lone whitebark pine, the smallish conifer of the high country. Young whitebarks and young lodgepoles look very similar; however, by the time a whitebark's trunk gets to be about 8″ thick, its bark is noticeably whiter than a lodgepole's.

Our steep trail begins to level off near the top of the ridge, and on this stretch the flower "collector" may add spreading phlox, red mountain heather, buckwheat and pennyroyal to his day's journal. Atop the ridge, the well-earned view includes, clockwise from north, Gaylor Peak, Tioga Peak, Mt. Dana, Mt. Gibbs, the canyon of the Dana Fork, Kuna Peak, Mammoth Peak, Lyell Canyon, and the peaks of the Cathedral Range. From our vantage point we can see where red metamorphic rocks to the northeast are in contact with gray granites to the southwest. This division extends north to where we are standing.

As we move west on the ridgetop, the rocks underfoot become quite purplish, a hue shared by the flowers of penstemon and lupine that obtain their mineral requirements from these rocks. Now our trail descends steeply past clumps of whitebark pine to Middle Gaylor Lake, and skirts the lake's north shore. Across the lake, the peaks of the Cathedral Range seem to be sinking into the lake, for their summits barely poke above the water.

Cathedral Range "rising" out of Middle Gaylor Lake

Taking the trail up the inlet stream, we begin a short, grad-
ual ascent to Upper Gaylor Lake. Surveying the Gaylor Lakes
basin, we can see that campsites are so few and wood so scarce
that only a few summers of camping, were it allowed, would
finish off the environment here. From the upper lake we can
see a rock cabin, which bespeaks the activities of a mining
company that sought to tap the silver veins that run somewhere under Tioga Hill, directly north of the lake. After picking our way up to the cabin, we marvel at the skill of the dry-
rock mason who built this long-lasting house near the Sierra
crest. Farther up the hill are other works—including one dangerous hole—left by the miners, in various states of return to
nature. This was once the "city" of Dana.

Atop Tioga Hill we have all the earlier views plus a view
down into Lee Vining Canyon. A scant mile northeast of us
another "city," Bennettville, sprang up near the mouth of a
tunnel being dug to exploit the silver lodes. Its founder project-
ed a population of 50,000! The white and lavender columbines

and other living things around the summit may owe their lives to the absence of these hordes.

From this general area, we make our way west cross country across a ridge and down to the easily found Granite Lakes, blue gems backed by steep granite heights. Like the upper lake with its near-shore island, lower Granite Lake is coldly swimmable in mid-to-late season. In any event, its grassy eastern shore is a fine place to sun oneself.

Finally we curve southwest, down toward Lower Gaylor Lake. In this meadowy upland we are sure to see many marmots and Belding ground squirrels. At Lower Gaylor Lake we are also likely to see a few California gulls on the spit. Spotted sandpipers, identified by their bobbing walk, are also common summer visitors to this quad's lakes. (Day Hike #11 describes the trail from Tuolumne Meadows Lodge northeast to here.) After a pleasant rest, we make an easy, generally open, cross-country climb northeast back to Middle Gaylor Lake, then follow the trail back to Tioga Pass.

DAY HIKE #13

Gardisky Lake

0.9 mile, or 1.4 km, one way (E1)

The trail to Gardisky Lake is easy to follow, though steep and exhausting to climb. Near timberline, it levels off, and then dies out about 200 yards before you reach the lake. The creek that the trail parallels up toward the lake drains from a shallow pond that is well worth investigating. Note that its rocky bottom is patterned with a network of polygonal stone rings. The process causing this pattern isn't completely understood, but it is known that repeated freezing and melting of ice over hundreds of years separates the coarse rocks from the finer particles. If you step in the middle of one of these polygons—usually a hexagon—you'll sink into clay. This phenomenon is not seen at many High Sierra ponds because they typically are found in granitic terrain. This pond, however, is in metamorphic terrain, and at high elevations like here, metamorphic rock is shattered by ice wedging, which breaks it into many small, unstable blocks.

You can extend your hike by making an enjoyable, view-packed excursion along the Tioga Crest, starting cross-country due north toward the saddle above Gardisky Lake. Shrubby whitebark pines and occasional noisy Clark nutcrackers are quickly left behind as you enter the alpine world. Some rare plant species exist along the crest, including the inch-high snow willow, which hugs the seemingly barren rocky ground in the Dore Pass area. To identify this and other plant species, take along Weeden's guide (see Recommended Reading)—the best Sierra plant guide available at any price. From broad Dore Pass—a relict land surface being attacked by glaciers—you can descend west, following the path of least resistance down to Saddlebag Lake.

Gardisky Lake

DAY HIKE #14

Saddlebag Lake Hinterlands

minimum distance from dam trailhead:
8.1 miles, or 13.1 km, semiloop trip (E1)

Just before Saddlebag Campground is a fairly large trailhead parking area for those hiking north into the Hoover Wilderness. You can get both a wilderness permit and fishing license at close-by Saddlebag Lake Resort. The resort's store sells fishing supplies and a few groceries, and its cafe serves breakfast and lunch—and evening meals to those who make reservations. The resort also rents boats, and on weekends Saddlebag Lake is often peppered with fishermen in pursuit of the lake's brook, rainbow and Kamloops trout. If you want to fish here, great, but get off this large lake in a hurry if a thunderstorm approaches—lightning kills. The resort also provides scenic trips on the lake plus water-taxi service to the lake's far end. In 1976 a round-trip taxi fare cost $2 per person and an additional $1.50 per backpack. This may be expensive for many, but the water taxi *does* pick you up at your own pre-arranged time.

To get to the lake's far end, you could hike along the closed road that parallels the east shore, but a better, shorter alternative is to hike on a trail that parallels the west shore. From the trailhead parking entrance you can see a road descending to the base of the lake's dam, then climbing to the dam's west end. Here the trail begins—a blocky tread cutting across open, equally blocky talus slopes. This metamorphic-rock talus may be uncomfortable to walk on, but from an alpine plant's perspective it is better than granitic-rock talus. Metamorphic bedrock fractures into smaller pieces than granitic bedrock does, thus creating a greater water-storage capacity for plants. Furthermore, it is much richer in dark minerals, so it makes a more nutrient-rich soil. And, being darker in color than their granitic counterparts, metamorphic-derived soils absorb heat—very important to plants at these alpine altitudes.

About ½ mile north of the dam, our trail bends northwest and Mt. Dana, in the southeast, disappears from view. Shepherd Crest, straight ahead, now captivates our attention, in tranquil reflection across the early morning waters of Saddlebag Lake. Among willows and a fiery field of Peirson's paintbrush, our trail dies out near the lake's north end, and we climb west to the east shore of Greenstone Lake. In the early morning a breathtaking reflection of North Peak mirrors across the placid waters, providing some of the best color-photography potential in this quadrangle. Following the lake's shore north, we quickly meet the closed mining road that water-taxi riders will be hiking west on. Above the lake's north shore, our narrow road enters the Hoover Wilderness, an area of 47,916 acres flanking the northeast boundary of Yosemite National Park. It serves as a buffer for the Park wilderness and is itself a

North Peak over Greenstone Lake

beautiful, if not more spectacular, piece of wilderness. Southwest across Greenstone Lake a granite wall sweeps up to a crest at Mt. Conness, in whose shade lies the largest glacier in the *Tuolumne Meadows* quadrangle. Our main tread, complicated by two short jeep-road segments, climbs northwest, and then at the "Z" Lake outlet creek bends west over to relatively warm Wasco Lake.

Beyond the first tarn north of Wasco Lake, our trail enters the drainage of northeast-flowing Lundy Creek. Just beyond the second tarn we come to a junction with a jeep trail—the start of interesting side trips. This trail descends north to the south shore of Steelhead Lake, bends west, then starts a climb south up a linear gully. Growing in its moist confines are dense clusters of Suksdorf's monkey flowers. Typical of many alpine plants, their stems are greatly reduced, thereby making their one-inch-long yellow flowers seem greatly oversized. You can continue up the gully, then branch southwest to an easily reached snowfield on North Peak, or you might climb west from the gully to nearby Potter Lake. This picturesque gem holds the distinction of having a small glacial erratic perched atop a giant one at the lake's whitebark-pine-fringed outlet. Its outlet creek immediately cascades noisily into deep Steelhead Lake, and near the cascade are ledges from which brave souls can high-dive into that lake's chilly depths. Finally, cross-country hikers can walk northwest from the cascade, quickly pass Towser Lake, then scramble west up a trail of sorts to Secret Lake, just below a crest. Experienced off-trail hikers can climb up to this crest, then descend steep slopes to fairly isolated Upper McCabe Lake.

Those keeping to the main route follow the closed jeep road north alongside deep blue Steelhead Lake to its outlet. The road continues west above the lake's north shore to the Hess Mine, blocked with boulders. Higher up the road, however, is an unblocked mine that goes 50 yards into the mountainside. Just beyond it the road ends and there you have a commanding view of this "20 Lakes Basin," as it is sometimes

North Peak over Steelhead Lake

called. The large, white horizontal dikes on North Peak stand
out well, and pointed Mt. Dana pokes its summit just into view
on the southeast skyline.

On the west side of Steelhead Lake's outlet—Mill Creek—we
go a few yards downstream, then scramble over a low knoll as
we follow a faint trail that quickly descends to the west shore
of tiny Excelsior Lake. At the north end we go through a
notch just west of a low metamorphic-rock knoll that is strewn
with granitic glacial erratics. A long, narrow pond quickly
comes into view which, like many of the lakes, contains trout.
Our trail skirts its west shore, then swings east to the north

shore of adjacent, many-armed Shamrock Lake, a good photo foreground for the giant Conness Glacier.

Our ducked route—more cross country than trail—now continues northeast over a low ridge, then goes past two Mill Creek ponds down to the west shore of Lake Helen. On a trail across talus we round this lake's north shore to Mill Creek, where our trail dies out just below the lake's outlet—which flows through a tunnel. We go 30 yards up to the tunnel, walk across it, and begin an east-shore traverse south across blocky talus. Adding warm colors to the dark metamorphic rocks are crimson columbines, white Coville's columbines and their pink hybrids. Two creeks empty into the lake's southeast end, and we follow the eastern one up a straight, narrow gully that in early season is a snow chute rather than a wildflower garden. Soon reaching the outlet of Odell Lake, we cross it and parallel the west shore southward while observing the lobes of talus just east of the lake. Like some other metamorphic-rock talus slopes in this glaciated basin, these developed lobes through solifluction—a slow downslope flowage of unstable, water-saturated rock masses.

Near the lake's south end our trail forks, and the older route climbs slightly before dying out while the newer route drops to water's edge before climbing from the south shore up to Lundy Pass. At this gap our path quickly disappears, but by heading south down toward a pond, we soon reach the outlet of Hummingbird Lake and here our trail resumes. This tread parallels the east side of the outlet creek ½ mile down to the closed mining road. Here you can descend to the water-taxi dock and wait for the boat if you made reservations for a return trip, or you can retrace your steps on the west shore trail. Of course, for variety you can take the closed road back to the lake's south end.

"All intellectual improvement arises from leisure."
Samuel Johnson

MAIN TRAIL #1

John Muir Trail Westbound

15.7 miles, or 25.3 km, to Little Yosemite Valley (C3)

From the Budd Creek Trailhead, we follow a gently ascending trail that is quite objectionably dusty except after rain sprinkles. After this initial section, however, the trail itself is not bad at all, and the panoramic views more than make up for the early unpleasantness. A few minutes from the trailhead our route crosses the Tenaya Lake/Tuolumne Meadows Trail and then begins to climb more steeply. After ¾ mile of ascent under a welcome forest cover, the trail levels off and descends to a small meadow that is boggy in early season. From here we can see the dramatically shaped tops of Unicorn Peak and the Cockscomb, and in the south the apparent granite dome is really the north ridge of Cathedral Peak, whose steeples are out of sight over the "dome's" horizon.

Our viewful trail continues to cruise gently up and down through more little meadows set in hemlock forest, and then dips near a tinkling stream whose source, we discover after further walking, is a robust spring on a shady set of switchbacks. Beyond this climb our tread levels off on the west slope of Cathedral Peak and makes a long, gentle, sparsely forested descent on sandy underfooting to a junction with the spur trail to lower Cathedral Lake. Many hikers go no farther on the John Muir Trail, but rather follow this spur trail ¾ mile down to the lake's bedrock east shore. A rust-stained waterline on the meadow side of the bedrock marks the high-water level when the meadow floods in early season. The iron for the rust is derived from the meadow's soil, not from the iron-deficient granitic bedrock. Campsites abound on both the north and south shores, the northern ones being roomier. As do all popular Yosemite lakes, this one attracts black bears.

Perhaps after a swim in the relatively warm waters, return to the John Muir Trail and make an easy mile-long climb to the southeast corner of very shallow upper Cathedral Lake. Although camping is now discouraged here, you may enjoy a stop for a snack on the south-shore peninsula, from which you can at times get good mirrored-image photos of two-towered Cathedral Peak. Our trail then climbs ¼ mile to broad Cathedral Pass, where the excellent views include Tresidder Peak, Cathedral Peak, Echo Peaks, Matthes Crest, the Clark Range farther south, and Matterhorn Peak far to the north.

Beyond the pass is a long, beautiful swale, the headwaters of Echo Creek, where the midseason flower show is alone worth the trip. Our path traverses up the east flank of Tresidder

Cathedral Peak from Upper Cathedral Lake

Columbia Finger from Long Meadow

Peak on a gentle climb to the actual high point of this trail, at
a marvelous viewpoint overlooking most of southern Yosemite
Park. The inspiring panorama here includes the peaks around
Vogelsang High Sierra Camp in the southeast, the whole Clark
Range in the south, and the peaks on the Park border in both
those directions farther away. Our high trail soon traverses
under steep-walled Columbia Finger, then switchbacks quickly
down to the head of the upper lobe of Long Meadow. Here it
levels off and leads down a gradually sloping valley dotted
with little lodgepole pines to the head of the second, lower
lobe of l-o-n-g Long Meadow. After passing a junction with a
trail down Echo Creek, the route heads south ½ mile before
bending west ¼ mile to pass below Sunrise High Sierra Camp,
perched on a granite bench just above the trail. South of the
camp are some backpacker campsites from where you can take
in the next morning's glorious sunrise.

The trail continues through the south arm of Long Meadow, then soon starts to climb up the east slopes of Sunrise Mountain. You top a broad southeast-trending ridge, and then, paralleling the headwaters of Sunrise Creek, descend steeply by switchbacks down a rocky canyon. At the foot of this descent you cross a trickling creek, then climb a low moraine to another creek, and in a short ½ mile top the linear crest of a giant lateral moraine. This moraine is the largest of a series of ridgelike glacial deposits in this area, and the gigantic granite boulders along its sides testify to the power of the glacier that once filled Little Yosemite Valley and its tributary valleys. Most of the rocks have decomposed to soil—an indication of the moraine's old age. More morainal crests appear on both sides of the trail and Half Dome is seen through the trees be-

Matthes Crest from Sunrise Camp

fore our route reaches a junction with the Forsyth Trail (Lateral Trail #4). There are fair campsites on Sunrise Creek about 150 yards north of this junction.

Here we turn south and in a moment reach the "High Trail" (Lateral Trail #1) coming in on the left. Turning right, we descend southwest, as our path is bounded on the north by giant cliffs—the south buttress of the Clouds Rest eminence— and on the south by Moraine Dome. Where our trail bends west, sharp-eyed hikers may see a shallow saddle ¼ mile south of them, which lies at the foot of the dome. From this saddle they can follow the crest of a lateral moraine northeast up to the dome's summit. This moraine, hanging on the south side of Moraine Dome about 1750 feet above the floor of Little Yosemite Valley, represents the approximate thickness of the largest of three glaciers that descended the Merced River canyon in the last 100,000 years. The last of these three glaciers, retreating upcanyon only 10,000 years ago, never extended downcanyon beyond the western portion of Little Yosemite Valley, contrary to earlier beliefs. Atop Moraine Dome you'll see—besides an utterly fantastic panorama—several geologically interesting features. One is a seven-foot-high dike of resistant aplite, which stands above the rest of the dome's surface because it weathers more slowly. Nearby just downslope is a large glacial erratic boulder which, unlike the rock of Moraine Dome, is composed of Cathedral Peak granodiorite, easily identified by its large feldspar crystals. The very ancient glacier that left this erratic here also leveled the aplite dike to the dome's surface, but, as you can see, in the eons of ensuing time the dome has eroded both *around* the slowly weathering dike and *beneath* the erratic, leaving it perched precariously atop a three-foot-high pedestal.

A mile from the last junction, the John Muir Trail (now off the *Tuolumne Meadows* map) fords Sunrise Creek in a red-fir forest whose stillness is broken by the creek's gurgling and by the occasional screams of Steller jays. In ¾ mile from the ford we see a good campsite on a large, shady creekside flat, then curve northeast to quickly cross the creek's tributary, which has two west-bank campsites. Immediately past these is a trail to Clouds Rest, and ½ mile west from this junction we meet the trail to Half Dome (about 4 miles round trip—an incredible hike that shouldn't be missed). From this junction our shady path switchbacks down through a changing forest cover that includes some stately incense-cedars, with their burnt-orange, fibrous bark. At the foot of this descent there are some improved campsites on Sunrise Creek, and more numerous ones ¼ mile south, along the Merced River south of the river trail. Here in Little Yosemite Valley, the campsites are swarmed on weekends by both backpackers and bears. Be sure to bearbag your food. (The route from here to Yosemite Valley is described in the High Sierra Hiking Guide to the *Yosemite* quadrangle.)

Black bear cubs practice climbing

MAIN TRAIL #2

John Muir Trail Eastbound

12.7 miles, or 20.4 km, to Donohue Pass (D3)

The trailhead is beside the west end of the Tuolumne Meadows Lodge parking lot—although you will have to take your car back to one of the backpacker parking lots west of here on the Lodge spur road. The route goes about 100 yards to the Dana Fork of the Tuolumne River and crosses it on a sturdy bridge. Just upstream we meet a trail to Gaylor Lakes branching left, upriver. From here the John Muir Trail leads over a slight rise and descends to the Lyell Fork, where there are two substantial bridges. The meadows above these bridges are among the most delightful in all the Sierra, and anytime you happen to be staying all night at the lodge or nearby, they are a wonderful place to spend the last hour before dinner. Mt. Dana and Mt. Gibbs fill the eastern horizon, catching the late sun, and the river has good fishing for brown trout.

About 70 yards past the bridges we meet the trail that comes up the river from the Tuolumne Meadows campground, turn left (east) onto it, and skirt a long, lovely section of the meadow. This re-routed trail was established because of extensive wear and ensuing erosion of the old route. Re-routing is one of several far-sighted Park Service policies that have been adopted to allow areas in wilderness a "breather"—a chance to recover from overuse. Going through a dense forest cover of lodgepole pine, our route passes the trail to Vogelsang High Sierra Camp (Main Trail #7) and then fords two branches of Rafferty Creek. The first ford may be difficult in early season.

East of the creek the trail traverses alternating wet-meadow and forest section—with some of the worst mosquito clouds to be found anywhere—then veers southward, climbing between two resistant granite outcrops. The silent walker may come upon grazing deer in the meadows and an occasional marmot

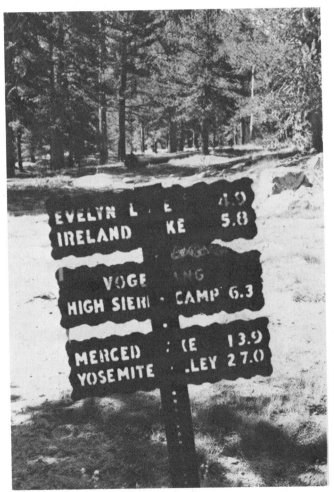

that has ventured from the rocky outcrops. Fields of wildflowers color the grasslands from early to late season, but the best time of the year for seeing this color is usually in July. From the more open parts of the trail, one has excellent views of the Kuna Crest as it slopes up to the southeast, and the river itself has delighted generations of mountain photographers.

After an hour of easy, nearly level walking, our Lyell Canyon route passes a trail branching southwest to Evelyn Lake and Vogelsang High Sierra Camp, (Lateral Trail #3), with many campsites around the junction. Beyond, the trail fords multibranched Ireland Creek, passes below Potter Point, and ascends gently for three miles to the fair campsites at Lyell Base Camp, just beyond cascading Kuna Creek. This camp, sur-

Lyell Fork, Potter Point

rounded on three sides by steep canyon walls, marks the end of the meadowed sections of Lyell Canyon, and is the traditional first-night stopping place for those touring the Muir Trail south from Tuolumne Meadows.

From Lyell Base Camp the trail ascends the steep southern terminal wall of Lyell Canyon to a granite bench. On it we pass a few campsites just before the confluence of the Maclure Creek tributary of the Lyell Fork. Then our route crosses the bridge to the east side and switchbacks up to some very used campsites among clumps of whitebark pines just before recrossing the fork at the north edge of a subalpine meadow. The rocky underfooting beyond the ford takes us up past the foot of superb alpine meadows, from where views of the glaciers on the north faces of Mt. Maclure and Mt. Lyell are superlative. Hikers who wish to obtain a more intimate view or to ascend to these ice fields via the lake-dotted basin at their feet should take the ducked route that leaves our trail where we turn east and recross the infant Lyell Fork at the north end of a boulder-dotted pond.

From this ford our trail winds steeply up rocky going and eventually veers southeast up a long, straight fracture to Donohue Pass (11056') at the crest of the Sierra and on the border of Yosemite Park. Just before and just after the pass—not at it —one has great views of the Sierra crest, composed of the Cathedral Range to the northwest and the Ritter Range to the southeast. (This trail description is continued in the High Sierra Hiking Guide to *Devils Postpile*.)

"In the eager search for the benefits of modern science and technology, we have been enticed into a nearly fatal illusion: that we have at last escaped from the dependence of man on the balance of nature." Barry Commoner

MAIN TRAIL #3

Tenaya Lake to Sunrise Camp

5.7 miles or 9.1 km, one way (A4)

From the campground parking lot, we follow a closed road that quickly crosses the outlet of Tenaya Lake via a ford, narrows to a trail, and then parallels this stream southwestward. In 150 yards we meet a trail that parallels Highway 120 northeast to Tuolumne Meadows. Our trail continues south for ¼ mile along the stream, then in sparse forest ascends southeast over a little rise and drops to a ford of Mildred Lake's outlet, which is dry in late season—like the three other streams shown on the topo map between Tenaya Lake and the Sunrise Trail junction.

Beyond the Mildred Lake stream our trail undulates and winds generally south, passing several pocket meadows where the quiet early-morning hiker may see mule deer browsing. The trail then begins to climb in earnest, through a thinning forest cover of lodgepole pine and occasional red fir, silver pine and mountain hemlock. As our trail rises above Tenaya Canyon, we pass several vantage points from which we can look back upon its polished granite walls, though we never see the lake. To the east the canyon is bounded by Tenaya Peak; in the northwest are the cliffs of Mt. Hoffmann and Tuolumne Peak.

Now on switchbacks, we can see the highway across the canyon and can even hear passing cars, but these annoyances are infinitesimal compared to the pleasures of polished granite expanses all around. These switchbacks are mercifully shaded, and where they become steepest, requiring a great output of energy, they give us back the beauty of the finest flower displays on this trail, including lupine, penstemon, Indian paintbrush, mountain aster, larkspur, buttercup and senecio. Finally the switchbacks end and the trail levels off as it arrives at a junction on a shallow, forested saddle.

Here we turn left, contour east, cross a low gap and descend momentarily north to lower Sunrise Lake, above whose east shore you'll see excellent examples of exfoliating granite slabs. The large talus slope beneath them testifies to the slabs' instability. Climbing from this lake and its small campsites, we reach a crest in several minutes, and from it one could descend an equally short distance north to more isolated, island-dotted middle Sunrise Lake. The trail, however, gains a very noticeable 150′ in elevation as it climbs east to upper Sunrise Lake, the largest and most popular lake of the trio. Campsites are plentiful along its north shore, away from the trail.

Leaving this lake, the trail climbs south up a gully, crosses it, then soon climbs up a second gully to the east side of a broad gap, from which we see the Clark Range head-on, piercing the southern sky. From the gap, which is sparsely clothed with mountain hemlocks, whitebark pines and silver pines, we descend south into denser cover, and veer east and then north to make a steep descent to Sunrise High Sierra Camp and the adjacent backpackers' campground. An overnight stay in this area is highly recommended, for it gives you an inspiring sunrise over Matthes Crest and the Cathedral Range.

Exfoliation at Middle Sunrise Lake

MAIN TRAIL #4

Tuolumne Meadows to May Lake

14.0 miles, or 22.6 km, one way (C3)

This trail is part of the High Sierra Camps Loop. As far as Glen Aulin, it is also a segment of the Pacific Crest Trail and the Tahoe-Yosemite Trail. Finally, the first mile-plus is part of the route to Young Lakes. Hence it figures in the descriptions of three "main trails."

From the Dog Lake parking area west of Highway 120 we stroll down a dirt road, pass a locked gate that bars autos, and continue west along the lodgepole-dotted flank of Tuolumne Meadows, with fine views south across the meadows of Unicorn Peak, Cathedral Peak and some of the knobby Echo Peaks. Approaching a boulder-rimmed old parking loop, we veer right and climb slightly past the old Soda Springs Campground, which once surrounded the still-bubbling natural soda springs. From here the sandy trail undulates through a forest of sparse, small lodgepole pines, and then descends to a boulder ford of Delaney Creek. Just before the ford, the stock trail from the stables back in the meadows comes in on the right. Immediately beyond the ford we hop a branch of Delaney Creek, hop another in 1/6 mile, and in 1/6 mile more pass the Young Lakes Trail (Main Trail #6).

At this junction our route goes left, and after more winding through scattered lodgepoles, it descends some bare granite slabs and enters level, cool forest. A half mile's pleasant walking in this shade brings us to the bank of the Tuolumne River, just before three branches of Dingley Creek, near the west end of the huge meadows. From here, the nearly level trail often runs along the river, and in these stretches by the stream, there are numerous glacier-smoothed granite slabs on which to take a sunny break.

After a mile-long winding contour, we climb briefly up a granite outcrop to get around the river's gorge. On the south

Right: Cathedral Range from down-river

side of the gorge below you is Little Devils Postpile, a dark plug of basalt that was forced up through the adjacent Cathedral Peak granite 9.4 million years ago. Despite repeated attacks by glaciers, this intrusion remains. Now we descend on individual stones carefully fitted together, down toward a sturdy bridge over the river. There are campsites on the south side of the river here, but these are illegal, since they are within four trail miles of Tuolumne Meadows. From these sites, however, you can hike upriver to Little Devils Postpile.

Immediately beyond the bridge we can look north up long Cold Canyon to Matterhorn Peak and Whorl Mountain, and, to their right, Mt. Conness. The trail then dips through several glades brightened by labrador-tea flowers and corn lilies. As the river approaches Tuolumne Falls, it flows down a series of sparkling rapids separated by large pools and wide sheets of water spread out across slightly inclined granite slopes. Beyond this beautiful stretch of river the trail descends, steeply at times, past Tuolumne Falls and the White Cascade to a junction with the trail to May Lake. From here it is only a few minutes' walk to Glen Aulin Camp, reached by crossing the river on a bridge below roaring White Cascade and the great green pool it plunges into.

Turning left at the junction, we curve northwest through a notch and then our duff trail ascends gently southwest, soon crossing and recrossing McGee Lake's *northeast*-flowing outlet, which dries up by late summer. Where the trail levels off, McGee Lake, long and narrow and bordered on the southwest by a granite cliff, comes into view through the lodgepole trees. The dead snags along the shallow margin, and the fallen limbs and downed trees make fishing difficult, and in late summer the lake may dwindle to a stale pond. Camping is best at its south end.

Beyond the lake our trail descends along its *southwest*-flowing outlet for ¾ mile, crosses this stream, and in ¼ mile reaches a tributary of Cathedral Creek. From here we have a view down the shallow granite canyon to hulking Falls Ridge, which

White Cascade

this creek has to detour around in order to join the Tuolumne River. A few hundred yards beyond this ford is a boulder-hop ford of 20-foot-wide Cathedral Creek, which runs all year. On the moderate ascent beyond the creek, we soon reach a stand of tall, healthy red firs, and the contrast with the small, over-crowded lodgepole pines earlier on the trail is inescapable.

Higher on the trail, there are good views, and after three miles of walking through moderate and dense forest, the panorama seems especially welcome. In the distant northeast stand Sheep Peak, North Peak and Mt. Conness, guarding the basin of Roosevelt Lake. In the near north, Falls Ridge is a mountain of pinkish granite that challenges the white and gray granite of the other peaks. When we look back toward McGee Lake, the route appears to be entirely carpeted with lodgepole pines.

Our trail continues up a moderate slope on gravel and granite shelves, through a forest cover of hemlock, red fir and lodgepole. After arriving at a branch of Cathedral Creek, we cross it, then more or less parallel it for almost a mile to a junction shaded under some tall hemlocks. A trail departs from this junction to go down Murphy Creek to Tenaya Lake. Down this trail, a short ½ mile before the lake, a lateral trail departs southwest, parallels Highway 120, and ends at a bend in the highway between the two Tenaya Lake Walk-in Camp-grounds.

A half mile from the hemlock-shaded junction, we pass a trail to Ten Lakes that climbs slopes beneath the very steep east face of Tuolumne Peak. Here we branch left and ascend briefly to a long, narrow, shallow, forested saddle beyond which large Tenaya Lake is visible in the south. After traversing somewhat open slopes of sagebrush, huckleberry oak and lupine, we reach a spring with a manmade water basin, then momentarily come to a series of switchbacks. Our progress up the long, gentle gradient of these zigzags is distinguished by the striking views of Mt. Conness, Mt. Dana and the other giants on the Sierra crest/Yosemite border. The trail then passes through a little saddle just north of glacier-smoothed

Peak 9161, and ahead, suddenly, is another Yosemite landmark, Clouds Rest, rising grandly in the south: we are looking
at part of the largest expanse of bare granite in the Park.

Now our trail descends gradually over fairly open granite to
a forested flat and bends west above the north shore of Raisin
Lake, which is one of the warmest "swimming holes" in this
quadrangle. It also has pleasant campsites, and some hikers
might want to purify the water. From the lake view, we walk
beside a flower-lined runoff stream bed under a sparse forest
cover of hemlock and silver and lodgepole pine, and then
swing west to ford three unnamed streams (if it's still early season; otherwise they will be dry).

Finally we begin the last ½-mile steep ascent of this trip on
a rocky trail up a slope sparsely dotted with red firs, silver
pines and other conifers. Views improve constantly as we
breathe more heavily, and presently we have a panorama of
the peaks on the Sierra crest from North Peak to Mt. Gibbs.
The Tioga Pass notch is clearly visible. At the top of this climb
is a gentle upland where several small meadows are strung
along the trail, with turgid corn lilies growing at an almost per-
ceptible rate in early season, while aromatic lupine commands
our attention later on. In the west, Mt. Hoffmann is entirely
dominant. A little awed by it, we swing south past the backpackers' campsites at the northeast corner of May Lake and
down along the east shore to the High Sierra Camp, where we
meet the trail of Day Hike #1.

"The sun and the moon and the stars would have disappeared long ago . . . had they happened to be within
the reach of predatory human hands."   Havelock Ellis

MAIN TRAIL #5

Tuolumne Meadows to Lower McCabe Lake

14.1 miles, or 22.6 km, one way (C3)

The last part of this route, from the Pacific Crest Trail to lower McCabe Lake, is not a highly used trail. Rather, most hikers continue northwest on the PCT. But just beyond the McCabe junction, the PCT leaves *Tuolumne Meadows* quad and enters *Matterhorn Peak* quad, so, staying within the present quad, this description goes to the lake.

For the route from Tuolumne Meadows to Glen Aulin, see Main Trail #4. The trail north from Glen Aulin first takes us up a moderate ascent on a long, sloping shelf. The sparse soil here supports only a few lodgepole and silver pines; higher on the slopes are western junipers, which seem to sprout right out of the rock. An occasional backward glance rewards the hiker with views of the White Cascade's plunging waters dropping to the alluvial valley of Glen Aulin. As our trail gains elevation via a series of switchbacks, the view back comes to include the very tops of Cathedral Peak's rocky spires peeking over the intervening ridge. This south-facing slope is generally dry and hot in mid-to-late season, and past the bloom of its wildflowers. The poor soil supports some ground cover of red mountain heather in the shade of hemlocks and lodgepoles.

About two hours' walk from Glen Aulin we come to the long meadow south of Elbow Hill. The stream here meanders through the meadow in large loops, and in late season there is almost no flow. The deeply cut banks, however, indicate a much heavier flow in earlier season. About two thirds of our way through this long meadow, we see an excellent example of the tendency of lodgepole pines to encroach upon meadows, their seeds taking root wherever the normally thick turf is broken. Beyond this invaded meadow and a much smaller one, the trail steepens as it enters a dense cover of mixed conifers and begins the 400-foot climb to the McCabe Lakes Trail junction. In the red fir and lodgepole and silver pines here, the alert hiker may see chickadees, juncos, warblers, flycatchers, woodpeckers, bluebirds, robins and evening grosbeaks. Finally the long, moderate climb from the Elbow Hill meadow ends, overlooking forest-hidden deep Virginia Canyon, at the McCabe Lakes Trail junction. (For a description of the trail north from here, see the High Sierra Hiking Guide to *Matterhorn Peak*.)

Here we leave the Tahoe-Yosemite/Pacific Crest Trail, climb northeast up a moralal ridge, and level out as we approach McCabe Creek. This creek we now parallel, seldom seeing it due to the thick forest of hemlocks and pines. After a mile our route zigzags southeast up along the outlet creek of lower McCabe Lake, eventually reaching campsites along its northwest shore. The best sites are across the outlet creek, but regardless of where you camp, you can experience dramatic sunsets as towering Sheep Peak basks in a warm alpenglow. Those looking for more-remote campsites can follow the lake's inlet creek up to the middle lake, at timberline. From it one can climb up a ridge and drop to exposed, alpine Upper McCabe Lake, which is more easily reached—at least by experienced mountaineers—from Saddlebag Lake (see reference in Day Hike #14).

Lower McCabe Lake

MAIN TRAIL #6

Young Lakes

14.5 miles, or 23.3 km,
semiloop to and from lowest lake's outlet (C3)

The first part of this trip follows the Glen Aulin "high-way," a heavily traveled path from Tuolumne Meadows to the High Sierra Camp down the Tuolumne River. From the Dog Lake parking area west of Highway 120 we stroll down a dirt road, pass a locked gate that bars autos, and continue west along the lodgepole-dotted flank of Tuolumne Meadows, with fine views south across the meadows of Unicorn Peak, Cathedral Peak and some of the Echo Peaks. Approaching a boulder-rimmed old parking loop, we veer right and climb slightly to

Cathedral Range from Young Lakes Trail

the now-closed Soda Springs Campground. Once this campground was the private holding of John Lembert, namesake of Lembert Dome. His brothers, who survived him, sold it to the Sierra Club in 1912, and for 60 years Club members enjoyed a private campground in this marvelous subalpine meadow. In 1972 the Club deeded the property to the National Park Service so that everyone could use it, but in 1976 the Service closed the campground.

From the effervescent Soda Springs, the sandy trail undulates through a forest of sparse, small lodgepole pines, and then descends to a ford of multibranched Delaney Creek. Beyond the creek, our trail almost touches the northwest arm of Tuolumne Meadows before ascending to the signed Young Lakes Trail. Turning right, we ascend slightly and cross a broad expanse of boulder-strewn, grass-pocketed sheet granite. An open spot affords a look south across broad Tuolumne Meadows to the line of peaks from Fairview Dome to the steeple-like spires of the Cathedral Range. After crossing the open, glacier-polished granite, our trail climbs a tree-clothed slope to a ridge and turns up the ridge for several hundred yards before veering down into the bouldery, shallow valley of Dingley Creek, an easy ford except in early season. About ¼ mile beyond this small creek, we jump across its west fork and then wind moderately upward in shady pine forest carpeted with a flower display even into late season. Senecio, daisies, lupine, squawroot and gooseberries all are colorful, but one's admiration for floral beauty concentrates on the delicate cream flower cups of Mariposa lily, with one rich brown spot in the throat of each petal. Near the ridgetop, breaks in the lodgepole forest allow us glimpses of the whole Cathedral Range, a foretaste of the magnificent panorama we will see on the return route.

On the other side of the ridge a new panoply of peaks appears in the north—majestic Tower Peak, Doghead and Quarry Peaks, the Finger Peaks, Matterhorn Peak, Sheep Peak, Mt. Conness, and the Shepherd Crest. From this high viewpoint a

moderate descent leads to a ford of a tributary of Conness
Creek, where more varieties of flowers decorate the green
banks of this icy, dashing stream. Immediately beyond it the
Dog Lake Trail meets ours, and we start a rollercoaster traverse
northeast through a forest of hemlock and pine. On a level
stretch of trail we cross a diminutive branch of Conness Creek,
and then switchback ¼ mile up to a plateau from where the
view is fine of the steep northwest face of Ragged Peak. After
rounding the edge of a meadow, we descend to the west shore
of lower Young Lake. There are both primitive and well-devel-
oped campsites along the north shore of this lake. At the lake's
northwest corner you can hop its outlet creek—a wet ford in
early season—and climb ¼ mile east to a junction. Here a short
lateral veers right to the only good campsite at small middle
Young Lake. If you keep left, you'll climb 1/3 mile up to a
broad, open crest, from where you can start cross country to
Mt. Conness or Roosevelt Lake. Most likely, however, you'll
want to make an easy, nearly level, open traverse southeast to
upper Young Lake.

    After retracing our steps to the Dog Lake Trail junction, we
turn left and ascend a sandy, boulder-scattered slope under a

Upper Young Lake, Ragged Peak

moderate lodgepole-and-hemlock forest cover. As the trail ascends, the trees diminish in density and change in species, to a predominance of whitebark pine, the highest-dwelling of Yosemite's trees. From the southwest shoulder of Ragged Peak the trail descends through a very large, gently sloping meadow. This broad, well-watered expanse is a wildflower garden in season, laced with meandering brooks. Species of paintbrush, lupine, and monkey flower in the foreground set off the marvelous views of the entire Cathedral Range, strung out on the southern horizon.

Near the lower edge of the meadow we cross the headwaters of Dingley Creek and then descend, steeply at times, some 300 feet through a moderately dense forest of lodgepoles and a few hemlocks to a seasonal creek. Then the trail follows a rolling course southeast in lodgepole forest, where the sandy soil sprouts thousands of prostrate little lupine plants. Beyond is a very large, level meadow above which the reddish peaks of Mt. Dana and Mt. Gibbs loom in the east. Delaney Creek meanders lazily through the sedges and grasses, and Belding ground squirrels pipe away. The Delaney Creek ford is difficult in early season, but shallower fords may be found upstream from the main ford.

After climbing over a little ridge, our route drops once more toward Tuolumne Meadows. Lembert Dome, the "first ascent" of so many visitors to Tuolumne Meadows, can be glimpsed through the trees along this stretch of trail. The trail levels off slightly before it meets the 400-yard lateral to Dog Lake, a worthwhile side trip. In a few minutes our route passes a junction with a trail that leads east along the north side of Dog Dome, the lower adjunct of Lembert Dome. We keep southwest, cross Dog Lake's outlet creek, and begin a 450-foot switchbacking descent that is terribly dusty due to the braking efforts of descending hikers on this overly steep section. At the bottom of the deep dust, the trail splits into two paths. The right one leads to the stables, the left one to the parking area where we started.

MAIN TRAIL #7

Tuolumne Meadows-Vogelsang Loop

28.4 miles, or 45.7 km, without any side trips (D3)

First, follow Main Trail #2 a short two miles to the Rafferty Creek Trail junction. Here our route turns right and immediately begins the toughest climb of this entire trip. Even so, the grade is moderate as often as it is steep, the trail is fairly well shaded by lodgepole pines, and the length of the climb is well under a mile. Then, as the ascent decreases to a gentle grade, we pass through high, boulder-strewn meadows that offer good views eastward to reddish-brown Mt. Dana and Mt. Gibbs, and gray-white Mammoth Peak. Soon the trail dips close to Rafferty Creek, and since this stream flows all year you can count on refreshment here. After two miles of near-creek hiking, the gently climbing trail passes above an orange snowcourse marker—one of several—near the edge of a large meadow and continues its long, gentle ascent through a sparse forest of lodgepole pines unmixed with a single tree of any other species. In the next mile we cross several seasonal creeks, reach an even larger meadow, and immediately veer right at a junction where the abandoned old trail up the meadow veers left. Our relocated trail up a cobbly hillside was built to allow the damaged meadow below to recover from the pounding of too many feet—people's and, especially, horses'. Finally the exclusive lodgepole pines allow a few whitebark pines to join their company, and these trees diminish the force of the winds that often sweep through Tuolumne Pass. Through breaks in this forest one has intermittent views of cliff-bound, dark-banded Fletcher Peak and Peak 11799 in the south. Then our path leaves the green-floored forest and leads out into an area of bouldery granite outcroppings dotted with a few trees. Around this granite and past these trees we wind down to the west side of saucer-shaped Tuolumne Pass, a major gap in the

Cathedral Range. Taking the signed trail to Vogelsang from the junction here, we follow a rocky-dusty path along a moderately steep hillside below which Boothe Lake and its surrounding meadows lie serene in the west.

Finally our trail makes a short climb, and we see the tents of Vogelsang High Sierra Camp spread out before us at the foot of Fletcher Peak's rock glacier. A few snacks may be bought here, or dinner or breakfast if you make a reservation. There are fair campsites beside Fletcher Creek, but better ones just northeast at Upper Fletcher Lake. Remember the bears that live here are always interested in your food.

Taking the Vogelsang Pass Trail from the camp, we descend slightly to ford Fletcher Creek on boulders and then begin a 600-foot ascent to the pass. The panting hiker is rewarded, as always in the Sierra, with increasingly good views. Fletcher Peak, with its dozens of good climbing routes, rises grandly on the left, far north is Mt. Conness, and Clouds Rest and then

Boothe Lake

Half Dome come into view in the west-southwest. The trail skirts above the west shore of Vogelsang Lake as we look down on the turfy margins and the large rock island of this timberline lake. Nearer the pass, views to the north are occluded somewhat, but expansive new views appear in the south: from left to right are Parsons Peak, Simmons Peak, Mt. Maclure, the tip of Mt. Lyell behind Maclure, Mt. Florence, and, in the south, the entire Clark Range, from Triple Divide Peak on the left to Mt. Clark on the right.

From Vogelsang Pass, which has clumps of windswept whitebark pines, the trail rises briefly northeast before it switchbacks steeply down into sparse lodgepole forest. Many small streams provide moisture for thousands of lupine plants, with their light blue, pea-family flowers. The singing of the unnamed outlet stream from bleak Gallison Lake becomes clear as the trail begins to level off, and then we reach a flat meadow, through which the stream slowly meanders. There is a fine campsite beside this meadow, though wood fires are illegal here. After proceeding down a rutted, grassy trail for several hundred yards, we cross the Gallison outlet, top a low ridge, and make a brief, steep, rocky descent that swoops down to the meadowed valley of multibraided Lewis Creek. In this little valley in quick succession we boulder-hop the Gallison outlet and then cross Lewis Creek on a log. In a few minutes we reach a lateral trail that makes a steep half-mile climb to Bernice Lake. At the lake, among dwarf bilberry, red mountain heather and stunted lodgepole and whitebark pines, you can find small, marginal campsites. Perhaps the lake's best use is as a treeline base camp for those who want to explore the snowfields and alpine lakes between here and Simmons Peak. The lake is also well-located for enjoying the sight of alpenglow on the Sierra crest.

In a short ½ mile from the Bernice Lake Trail junction, we cross a little stream, then descend to another equally small one as we wind ¼ mile through dense hemlock forest to a good campsite beside Florence Creek. This year-round creek cas-

Florence Creek cascade

cades spectacularly down to the camping area over steep granite sheets, and the water sounds are a fine sleeping potion if you should choose to camp here.

Leaving the densely shaded hemlock forest floor, our trail descends a series of lodgepole-dotted granite slabs, and Lewis Creek makes pleasant noises in a string of chutes not far away on the right. Then, where the creek's channel narrows, the traveler will find on his left a lesson in exfoliation: granite layers peeling like an onion. One is more used to seeing this kind of peeling on Yosemite's domes, but this fine example is located on a canyon slope. As the bed of Lewis Creek steepens to deliver the stream's water to the Merced River far below, so does the trail steepen, and our descent to middle altitudes reaches the zone of red firs and silver pines. After dipping beside the creek, the trail climbs away from it to a junction with the High Trail, which climbs south up to the east rim of the Merced River canyon. From here the Lewis Creek Trail, now out of earshot of the creek, switchbacks down moderately, sometimes steeply, under a sparse cover of fir, juniper and pine for one mile to a junction with the Fletcher Creek Trail. If you have an extra day to spend, you might descend to Merced Lake, then retrace your steps to here. Otherwise, turn right onto this path and descend on short switchbacks to a wooden bridge over Lewis Creek. Just 50 yards past it we reach a good campsite, and then the trail enters more open hillside as it climbs moderately on a cobbled path bordered with proliferating bushes of mountain whitethorn and huckleberry oak. Just past a tributary ½ mile from Lewis Creek, we have fine views of cataracts and waterfalls on Fletcher Creek where it rushes down open granite slopes, while sparsely vegetated Babcock Lake dome presents a dramatic backdrop. We then come very close to the creek before veering northeast and climbing, steeply at times, up dozens of short switchbacks composed of cobbling placed by trail crews. Here one has more good views of Fletcher Creek chuting and cascading down from the notch at the base of the granite dome before it leaps off a ledge in free fall. The few solitary pine trees on this otherwise blank dome testify to nature's extraordinary persistence.

At the notch our trail levels off and reaches the side trail to Babcock Lake. This ½ mile trail arcs west to nearby Fletcher Creek, where the old trail used to cross. You, however, now go 30 yards downstream to a bedrock slab, cross there, and follow the trail northwest up to a low ridge. From it the trail goes southwest, crosses a second low ridge, then reaches the lake's northeast end. Among fair lodgepole-shaded campsites by the southeast shore, the trail dies out roughly 70 yards short of the lake's tiny island. Better campsites are on the opposite shore. Suitable diving slabs are along both shores of this fairly warm lake.

From the Babcock junction, the sandy Fletcher Creek Trail ascends steadily through a moderate forest cover, staying just east of Fletcher Creek. After ¾ mile this route breaks out into the open and begins to rise more steeply via rocky switchbacks. From these zigzags one can see nearby in the north the outlet stream of Emeric Lake—though not the lake itself, which is behind a dome just to the right of the outlet's notch. If you wish to camp at Emeric Lake—and it's a fine place—leave the trail here, cross Fletcher Creek at a safe spot, follow up the outlet creek's west side and camp on the northwest shore of Emeric Lake. The next morning, circle the head of the lake and find a trail at the base of the low granite ridge at the northeast corner of the lake. Follow this trail ½ mile northeast to a scissors junction in Fletcher Creek valley.

If you choose not to camp at Emeric Lake, continue up the trail into a long meadow guarded in the west by a highly polished knoll and presided over in the east by huge Vogelsang Peak. When you come to the scissors junction, take the left-hand fork up the valley and follow this rocky-dusty trail through the forest fringe of the long meadow that straddles Fletcher Creek. This trail climbs farther from the meadow and passes northwest of a bald prominence that sits in the center of the upper valley of Fletcher and Emeric creeks, separating the

Fletcher Creek valley

two. After topping a minor summit, the trail descends slightly and then winds almost level past several lovely ponds that are interconnected in early season. Then, immediately beyond an abandoned section of old trail, there is a lakelet 100 yards in diameter that would offer good swimming in some years. Just beyond it, the old trail veers sharply right, and our rutted meadow trail, going left, traverses northeast to a little swale with another possible swimming pond before reaching an overlook and nearby campsite above Boothe Lake. Our trail contours along meadowy slopes just east of and above the lake, passing a junction with a rutted use trail down to the lake. About ¼ mile farther we pass a reunion of this trail and then in an equal distance climb gently up to Tuolumne Pass. Here is the junction with the trail to Vogelsang, from where we retrace our steps north back to Tuolumne Meadows.

MAIN TRAIL #8

Tuolumne Meadows to Nelson Lake

5.9 miles, or 9.4 km, one way (C3)

The first part of this trip is described as Day Hike #1. Once beyond Elizabeth Lake, you almost have the ensuing spectacular country to yourself on most days. You trek south through the meadows east of Elizabeth Lake, then enter a moderately dense forest cover of lodgepole interspersed with mountain hemlock. Here the trail climbs steeply, then moderately, then steeply again. A few hundred yards before you reach the ridge crest, you come (in most years) to a late-lingering snowbank, where the trail splits. If you go left, you will pass through a narrow gully between granite walls. If you go right, you will walk up a bare granite-sand slope. We recommend that if you have a full pack, you take the right trail going to Nelson Lake

Looking north from above Elizabeth Lake

and left one returning, because of some steep places on the left trail just beyond the crest.

Because of the close proximity of the Cockscomb, about one mile due west, the hiker has excellent views of that finlike spire from just beyond the left pass. Well named by Francois Matthes, this slender crest bears clear marks of the highest level reached by the ice of the last glacial episode. Its lower shoulders reveal the rounded, well-polished surfaces that betray glacial action, while the jagged, sharply etched summit shows no such markings. Further evidence of glacial action may be clearly seen on the steep descent into the head of long, typically U-shaped Echo Creek valley. The shearing and polishing action of the ice mass that slightly widened this linear valley is evident on the west-side cliffs.

About 1/3 mile from where the trail split, and several hundred yards beyond the crest, the forks come together again on a steep, tree-dotted ravine-cut hillside. As our route descends along winding, clear, meadowed Echo Creek for about 2 miles, the canyon floor is lush with wildflower growth. During mid-season the passerby can expect to see Davidson's penstemon, spreading phlox, senecio, red mountain heather, lupine and swamp whiteheads. At the end of the second large flat-floored meadow in this canyon our trail leaves Echo Creek, veers southeast up a low, rocky ridge, drops through sparse forest, and climbs east up a second ridge. You are almost at Nelson Lake before you can see your destination, meadow-fringed at the foot of imposing granite Peak 11282. Good campsites may be found on the southeast and southwest sides. A very worthwhile cross-county jaunt from Nelson Lake is the 1½-mile walk up the inlet stream to gemlike Reymann Lake, in a glacial cirque close under the dramatic cliffs of Rafferty Peak.

> "What the banker sighs for, the meanest clown may have — leisure and a quiet mind." Henry David Thoreau

MAIN TRAIL #9

High Sierra Camps Loop Trail

50.4 miles, or 81.2 km, loop trip (D3)

This hike is probably the most popular backpack trip in the area. The High Sierra Camps are conveniently spaced an easy day's hike apart, making an enjoyable six-day hike. You can start this hike from any of several Tuolumne Meadows trailheads, from the May Lake trailhead, or from the Tenaya Lake trailhead. Most people start from the parking lot 1/3 mile west of Tuolumne Meadows Lodge (High Sierra Camp). Walk west past the ranger station to the next parking lot. From it a wide trail—an abandoned road—continues west to cross High-way 120 to a third parking lot. From here you follow Main Trail #4, first to Glen Aulin High Sierra Camp and then to May Lake High Sierra Camp. From the lake you follow Day Hike #1, described in the opposite direction, south to the May Lake trailhead. From here you follow the paved road north-east for two minutes to where it is blocked off, then descend the abandoned dirt road southeast to Highway 120. Cross the highway and follow a trail which parallels this noisy route to the Tenaya Lake Walk-in Campground. Now follow Main Trail #3 to Sunrise High Sierra Camp.

Leaving the camp, tread the John Muir Trail a short mile, first east and then north to the Lateral Trail #1. Take this 6½ miles down Echo Creek to a trail junction, leave Lateral Trail #1, and descend ¾ mile to the Merced Lake Trail, in Echo Valley. Now in the *Merced Peak* quadrangle, you first pass through a burned-but-boggy area, then climb east past the Merced River's largely unseen, but enjoyable, pools to Merced Lake's west shore. Don't camp here, but rather continue past the north shore to Merced Lake High Sierra Camp and the adjacent riverside campground. The bear population here is incredibly high, but there are good places to hang your food. A nearly level mile hike east gets you to the Merced Lake Ranger Station and a trail junction. From it you struggle 1¼ miles northeast up to another trail junction, from where you quickly re-enter the *Tuolumne Meadows* quadrangle as you follow the second half of Main Trail #7 back to your Tuolumne Meadows trailhead. If you plan to visit Vogelsang High Sierra Camp, go right at the scissors junction near Emeric Lake and hike 2-1/3 miles northeast up to the camp.

The Tuolumne Canyon below Glen Aulin

LATERAL TRAIL #1

Echo Creek and The High Trail

9.4 miles, or 15.2 km, one way (B4)

This lateral makes a loop off the southeast side of the John Muir Trail between Tuolumne Meadows and Little Yosemite Valley, coming fairly close to Merced Lake in the process. At the junction of Main Trail #1 in Long Meadow, we turn left onto the signed Echo Creek Trail and ford the Long Meadow stream on boulders. The trail quickly switchbacks up to the top of a ridge that separates this stream from Echo Creek and then descends through dense hemlock-and-lodgepole forest toward the Cathedral Fork of Echo Creek. Where our route approaches this stream, we have fine views of the creek's water gliding down a series of granite slabs, and then the trail veers away from the creek and descends gently above it for more than a mile. Even in late season this shady hillside is watered by numerous rills that are bordered by still-blooming flowers. On this downgrade the trail crosses the Long Meadow stream, which has found an escape from that meadow through a gap between two large domes high above our trail.

Our route then levels out in a mile-long flat section of this valley where the wet ground yields a plus of wildflowers all summer but a minus of many mosquitos in early season. Beyond this flat "park" the trail descends a more open hillside, and where it passes the confluence of the two forks of Echo Creek, we can see across the valley the steep course of the east fork plunging down to its rendezvous with the west fork. Finally the trail levels off and reaches the good campsites just before a metal bridge over Echo Creek.

Beyond the bridge, our trail leads down the forested valley and easily fords a tributary stream, staying well above the main creek. This pleasant, shaded descent soon becomes more open and steep, and it encounters fibrous-barked juniper trees and butterscotch-scented Jeffrey pines as it drops to another metal bridge one long mile from the last one. Beyond this sturdy span, the trail rises slightly and the creek drops precipitously, so that we are soon far above it, then our sandy tread swings west away from Echo Creek and diagonals down a brushy hillside. There the views are excellent of Echo Valley, which is a wide place in the great Merced River canyon below. On this hillside we arrive at a junction with the High Trail and turn right onto it. (For trails south of here see the High Sierra Hiking Guide to *Merced Peak*.)

This path climbs rockily several hundred feet before leveling off above the immense river canyon. This trail segment was part of the route from Yosemite Valley to Merced Lake until a path up the canyon was constructed in 1931. Before that, the steep canyon walls coming right down to the river near Bunnell Point—the great dome to our southwest—had made passage impossible. Finally a trail was built that bypasses the narrowest part of the canyon by climbing high on the south wall, and the trail we are now on fell into relative disuse.

With fine views of obelisklike Mt. Clark in the south, we descend gradually for ½ mile over open granite in a setting that is sure to give you a feeling of being above almost everything. The trail then passes a stagnant lakelet and ascends to even better viewpoints for appreciating the grandeur of the glaciated granitic wonder of nature spread out before you. It takes time to grasp the immensity of Mt. Clark, Clouds Rest, Half Dome, Mt. Starr King, Bunnell Point and the great unnamed dome across the canyon west of it. Our continuing ascent then rounds a ridge and veers north into a forest of handsome Jeffrey pines. Here the trail levels off, and it remains level for a mile of exhilarating walking through Jeffreys, lodgepoles and white firs which shade patch after patch of vivid green ferns and a complement of multihued floral displays. Still in forest, we climb slightly to meet the John Muir Trail. About 150 yards up it is the south end of the Forsyth Trail (Lateral Trail #4).

LATERAL TRAIL #2

Ten Lakes Trail

9.9 miles, or 16.0 km, to easternmost lake (A3)

This seldom used trail, involving a lot of climbing, provides a very long back-door route to the Ten Lakes Basin. It therefore is desirable only for those seeking solitude in the South Fork Cathedral Creek canyon. Starting in a forest dominated by mountain hemlocks, we leave Backpack Trail #4 and go ¼ mile southwest before veering north. Lodgepole pines, red firs and silver pines increase in numbers as we progress north, then thin out as we gain altitude, obtaining fair views east toward the Cathedral Range as we do. Moderately graded switchbacks take us up to a crest saddle—a good breather stop—and then we continue up a ridge to a higher crest. A tortuous traverse now confronts us as we first drop immediately to a sparkling pond—a good lunch spot—drop some more, then climb and drop and wind westward to a good overlook point high above the South Fork canyon.

Polly Dome, Tenaya Lake, Tenaya Peak

Short rocky switchbacks carry you down toward the canyon floor, and then you veer south on a long contour just below a low-angle cliff, only to resume more switchbacks. The South Fork is reached in minutes, and hiking down along it, one can find suitable campsites on either side of this creek. After two miles of near-creek winding trail, you cross this creek—a wet ford in early season—go briefly downstream, then prepare for a two-dozen-switchback climb of a generally open, juniper-dotted slope. Your last chance for secluded camping is in this vicinity, just downstream from the trail.

As you perspire up the switchbacks, stop and rest and take in the ever-expanding views of northern Yosemite, from Mt. Gibbs westward, with the north wall of the mighty gorge of the Tuolumne River dominating the foreground. As the switchbacks abate, the trail enters forest shade and then climbs ¾ mile to the quadrangle's edge, by then easing up in gradient and quickly attaining a shady crest. On it we walk ½ mile southwest, passing a small pond before crossing a broad saddle. Beyond it, about 150 feet below us, is the large eastern lake of the Ten Lakes Basin—an area with abundant potential for camping and exploration (see the High Sierra Hiking Guide to *Hetch Hetchy*).

LATERAL TRAIL #3

Vogelsang Camp to Lyell Canyon

6.5 miles, or 10.5 km, one way (D4)

You can make a very enjoyable 20½ mile (33 km) weekend hike by combining this trail with the trail up Rafferty Creek and the trail down Lyell Canyon. Starting either from Tuolumne Meadows Lodge or Toulumne Meadows Campground you can reach any of the six named lakes of the Fletcher Peak/Tuolumne Pass area in five hours or less. The first part of Main Trail #7 describes the route up to Vogelsang High Sierra Camp.

Leaving this near-timberline camp, we strike northeast, soon reaching popular Upper Fletcher Lake. From its northeast shore you can scramble cross country east up to larger Townsley Lake. The shortest route to large, orbicular Ireland Lake is to climb northeast from Townsley Lake to a large, broad plateau, strike east across it, and climb up to a long ridge north of Peak 11440+. From this ridge the descent southeast to Ireland Lake is obvious.

Our trail, however, leaves Upper Fletcher Lake, climbs steadily up to an indeterminable drainage divide, eases its gradient and passes through a flat-floored gully whose walls contain large, blocky feldspar crystals so typical of Cathedral Peak granodiorite. Beyond the gully a far-ranging view opens before us and on a large flat below us lies spreading, shallow, windswept Evelyn Lake, to whose outlet we now descend. Hikers who would like to try a slightly adventurous alternative to the Lyell Canyon Trail as a route back to Tuolumne Meadows can leave the trail at this outlet and stroll down the west slope of

Evelyn Lake seen from its outlet

this creek's canyon. You will pass through a beautiful, large, secluded meadow and walk beside delightful sections of the unnamed stream. Eventually, you will find, on the west side of the stream, a cliff which gradually diminishes in height. When the height has diminished to about 10 feet, find a place to scramble up the cliff and then walk a few hundred feet west to find the well-worn Rafferty Creek Trail.

Leaving desolate Evelyn Lake and its population of Belding ground squirrels, we stroll east, then climb through an open forest of stunted whitebark pines before dropping to a smaller, unnamed lake. Though higher than Evelyn Lake, it has some whitebark pines nearby, providing protection from the wind for those who would camp here. About a ½ mile climb northeast from this shallow lake takes us up to a low point on a long north-south crest. We have now left the Cathedral Peak pluton (a large, granitic body) behind and tread upon another pluton—one that lacks the conspicuous feldspar crystals.

Descending from this view-packed crest and its brushy whitebark pines, we follow a trail segment that contorts down slab after bedrock slab, soon bringing us to a junction with the 1½ mile-long Ireland Lake Trail. Lying beneath both granitic and metamorphic peaks, this large alpine lake is unsuited for camping unless you've brought along a tent to protect you from the wind.

Starting east from the trail junction, we soon descend gently south for ½ mile, then angle northeast to make a long two-mile descent that usually stays within earshot of Ireland Creek. Starting first along this creek's tributary, we are in a dense forest of lodgepole and whitebark pines, but the latter give way before we reach the flat floor of Lyell Canyon. This descent could be more enjoyable if the trail were not so steep. On the floor of Lyell Canyon our trail ends at Main Trail #2, which has many trailside campsites in this part of the canyon. The walk back to Tuolumne Meadows through this nearly level canyon is very easy—good therapy for the knee-knocking descent we've just completed.

LATERAL TRAIL #4

From the Clouds Rest Trail to the John Muir Trail

2.5 miles, or 4.1 km, one way (A4)

From the Clouds Rest Trail (Day Hike #3) we turn sharply left to meander over gravelly, nearly level ground. After winding eastward ½ mile, the trail starts its 1150-foot plunge down to Sunrise Creek. This switchbacking descent is a little tough on the knees, but in repayment the green fir-and-pine forest is a classic of its kind, and occasional views down into the Merced River Canyon are sweeping in their range. Finally our trail crosses a brook, follows it down to Sunrise Creek, and parallels this stream 1/3 mile before crossing to the fair campsites on the far bank. After a brief westward stroll along Sunrise Creek's south bank, our trail makes an equally brief climb south across a lateral moraine to reach its junction with the John Muir Trail (Main Trail #1).

Tenaya Lake

LATERAL TRAIL #5

Glen Aulin to Waterwheel Falls

3.4 miles, or 5.5 km, one way (B2)

To get the maximum enjoyment out of this trail, hike it in early summer, when the river's cascades are at their peak. Starting from Glen Aulin High Sierra Camp, we see the White Cascade, which tumultuously splashes into a swirling pool. The camp's sandy beach bordering the pool is periodically built up with fresh sand and gravel at times of very high runoff. Just 15 yards past the entrance to the camp, our lateral trail leaves the northbound Cold Canyon trail and climbs over a low knoll that sports rust-stained metamorphic rocks. From it we get an excellent view west down the flat-floored, steep-walled canyon. It looks like a glaciated canyon should look: U-shaped in cross section. However, the flat, broad Tuolumne Meadows vicinity upstream and the V-shaped Grand Canyon of the Tuolumne River downstream were also glaciated and are certainly not U-shaped. In this quadrangle it is the joint (fracture) pattern of the resistant granitic bedrock that determines the canyon's shape, not the process of glaciation, which in weaker rocks determines the shape.

Leaving the knoll, we switchback quickly down into Glen Aulin proper. Paralleling the Tuolumne River through a lodge-pole-pine forest, we pass several campsites that are popular with both hikers and bears. If you plan to camp here, you might consider storing your food at the High Sierra Camp even though they charge you for this service. We tread the gravelly flat floor of the glen for more than a mile, pass through a third gate, and then, on bedrock, quickly arrive at the brink of cascading California Falls, perched at the base of a towering cliff. Switchbacking down beside the cascade, we leave behind the glen's thick forest of predominantly lodgepole pines with associated red firs and descend past scattered Jeffrey pines and

California Falls

junipers and through lots of brush. At the base of the cascade, lodgepoles and red firs return once more as we make a gentle descent north. Near the end of this short stretch we parallel a long pool, which is a good spot to break for lunch or perhaps take a swim. However, stay away from the pool's outlet, where the Tuolumne River plunges over a brink.

Our trail parallels this second cascade as it generally descends through brush and open forest. On this descent we notice that red firs have yielded to white firs. Sugar pines also put in their first appearance as we reach the brink of broad Le Conte Falls, which cascades down fairly open granite slabs. Where we reach the flat-floored section of canyon, incense-cedar joins the ranks of white fir, Jeffrey pine and sugar pine, with few, if any, lodgepoles to be found. In this stand we quickly reach our fourth and final cascade, extensive Waterwheel Falls. This cascade gets its name from the curving sprays

Waterwheel Falls

of water thrown up into the air, which occur when the river is flowing with sufficient force. It is worth the trip in early season to see the white water turning to rainbow as it sprays the canyon full of light and color.

During the last major glacial period, which ended about 10,000 years ago, the Tuolumne Canyon glacier terminated at or just below this cascade. At best it reached Return Creek. However, during the previous glaciation, which ended about 40,000 years ago, a glacier flowed several miles farther down-canyon and was joined by glaciers flowing down both Matterhorn and Virginia canyons.

Although we suggest you stop here at the brink of the cascade, or better still down at the base of the cascade, you can hike all the way to Hetch Hetchy Reservoir (see *Hetch Hetchy High Sierra Hiking Guide*). From the brink of Waterwheel Falls the trail goes about 3½ miles to the quad's edge. Along this lower stretch you'll hike through a forest that contains gold-cup oak, black oak, Douglas-fir, cottonwood and dogwood. During the summer it is hot and fly-infested. On the map Return Creek looks like a good cross-country tour, but in reality it is overgrown with huckleberry oak and other shrubs, making an ascent up it a hot, dusty, exhausting experience.

OTHER HIKING SUGGESTIONS

In addition to the preceding trail descriptions, here are a few more hiking possibilities.

A. Yosemite Valley via Snow Creek (A4). This is the shortest of three routes from Tenaya Lake to the east end of Yosemite Valley. You can start it by paralleling Highway 120 west or by taking a meadowy path southwest from the walk-in campground. Good views of Clouds Rest and Half Dome are seen. This route is described in the *Hetch Hetchy* High Sierra Hiking Guide.

B. Tenaya Lake-Tuolumne Meadows Trail (C3). This well-maintained trail starts from the Budd Creek trailhead and more or less parallels Highway 120 southwest 8½ miles to the Tenaya Lake Walk-in Campground. It passes many domes, but these are hardly seen due to the thick cover of lodgepoles and hemlocks that block the views. It is good for easy exercise and for solitude, but otherwise has little to offer.

C. Pothole Dome (C3). From Tuolumne Meadows' western-most turnout, many people scramble up well-named Pothole Dome. You'll also see large, blocky feldspar crystals in the granodiorite bedrock, some of them up to four inches long. The dome provides an overview of Tuolumne Meadows that is second only to Lembert Dome's overview, and it also provides photogenic early-morning views of Fairview Dome and the peaks of the western part of the Cathedral Range.

D. Trails southeast from Dana Meadows (E3). Mono Pass and Parker Pass lie just east of this quadrangle, and trails to and beyond them are fully described in the *Mono Craters* High Sierra Hiking Guide.

E. Mt. Dana (E2). The trail east up Mt. Dana—Yosemite's second-highest peak—starts at Tioga Pass and is described in the *Mono Craters* High Sierra Hiking Guide.

F. Dana Lake, Dana Glacier, Dana Plateau (E2). A cross-country route, heavily used by mountaineers hiking up to the Dana Glacier, begins at a highway turnout above the south shore of

Tioga Lake and ascends Glacier Canyon. The views from Dana Plateau—a very old, pre-glacial land surface—rival, if not exceed, those from Mt. Dana. See the *Mono Craters* High Sierra Hiking Guide.

G. Tioga Tarns Nature Trail (E2). This trail starts from Highway 120 at a turnout about 1/3 mile northeast of the Tioga Lake Campground entrance. If you're camped in this area, you might stroll along this trail in the evening and capture Mt. Dana's alpenglow reflected in one of the tarns. Rocks, glaciers, plants and history are mentioned in simple terms on signs.

H. Carnegie Institute Experimental Station (E1). Not used much today, this station is reached by taking the closed road, on your left, ½ mile past the Gardisky Lake trailhead.

During most of the 1920s and 30s, environmental and genetic research was done at this station, at Mather (on Yosemite's border near Hetch Hetchy), and at Stanford University. Native Plants found at each location were transplanted to the two other locations to see the effect, if any, a different environment had on them. The study showed that each plant species will modify its shape and physiology to a certain extent in a new environment, but that each is best suited to survival in its native environment. These modifications are not passed on to future generations, and furthermore, when the plant is returned to its native environment, it resumes its natural state. However, mutations in plant genes can produce modifications that may be suitable for a different environment, thus giving a mutant plant an advantage over others of its kind, and these modifications *can* be passed onto future generations. Thus plants are able to adapt to changing climates and landscapes.

To the west and south of the station site lie over a dozen lakes and many snowfields, most reached by easy cross-country jaunts. The geology, flora and scenery here are perhaps the best in the whole quadrangle yet there are few people who see it. Many of the lakes in this Lee Vining watershed were named by Gardisky, an early trapper.

Climbers

THE *TUOLUMNE MEADOWS* AREA has about the best difficult, roped climbing to be found anywhere in the world. However, it is not as famous as Yosemite Valley, which has long been recognized as one of the world's great climbing centers. Perhaps this relative anonymity is good, for there are fewer routes in this area than in the Valley. Many climbers prefer the Tuolumne Meadows climbing, for it is cleaner, since there is very little dirt, loose rock or vegetation. The routes are often very spartan, with a minimal amount of holds, much to the consternation of climbers new to this area. The reason for this smoothness is that glaciers polished this granite as recently as 10,000 years ago, whereas down in the Valley the last glaciers to polish its *lower* cliffs did so 40,000 years ago. Many of the Valley routes haven't been cleaned by glaciers for 60,000 years or more. However, large protruding feldspar crystals, typically found in much of the Tuolumne Meadows' granitic rocks, do help to make many of its climbing routes easier.

Cathedral Peak

The great majority of these routes are Class 5 in difficulty; that is, they require ropes, climbing nuts and carabiners to catch the climber should he fall. The two steep cracks on the southwest face of Lembert Dome are good examples of Class 5 difficulty. Class 4 is considerably easier, yet a rope is generally used for safety. Class 3 is difficult scrambling, using hands and feet, but rarely using a rope. The exposed ledge system just east of the two cracks on Lembert Dome is a good example of this class of difficulty. Most of this guide's readers will be doing only Class 1 and 2 climbing. Class 2 is easy scrambling with occasional use of hands and Class 1 is trail and/or easy cross-country. Named summits with one or more routes that are Class 1 or Class 2 are listed below. You'll find these and the more difficult routes described in Roper's guide (see **Recommended Reading**).

Amelia Earhart Peak	North Peak	Simmons Peak
Conness, Mt.	Parsons Peak	Tenaya Peak
Fletcher Peak	Pettit Peak	Tioga Peak
Gaylor Peak	Potter Point	Tuolumne Peak
Johnson Peak	Rafferty Peak	Vogelsang Peak
Kuna Crest	Ragged Peak	West Peak
Mammoth Peak	Regulation Peak	Wildcat Point

If you have never climbed more difficult peaks but want to learn, the Yosemite Mountaineering and Guide Service will give you an opportunity to enjoy Yosemite's unrivaled alpine environment on a completely new plane of experience. The service conducts basic, intermediate and advanced rock-climbing classes, and also backpacking instruction, backpacking-climbing tours and special seminars. The service makes its summer home at the Mountain Sports Center, 0.8 mile west of the gas station in Tuolumne Meadows. The spring and late-summer headquarters is in the Mountain Shop in Yosemite Valley. For information write to Yosemite Mountaineering, Yosemite CA 95389.

CAMPGROUNDS, SERVICES AND ACTIVITIES

Campgrounds (listed from southwest to northeast)

Tenaya Walk-in Campground. Two adjacent campgrounds near the south shore of Tenaya Lake. All trails in this area converge at the south campground.

Tuolumne Meadows Campground. Larger than all other campgrounds in the quadrangle combined. Entrance at Information Center, immediately south of Tuolumne River bridge.

Tioga Lake Campground. On northwest shore of Tioga Lake, 1¼ miles north of Tioga Pass.

Junction Campground. Just 0.1 mile from Highway 120 on the Saddlebag Lake Road.

Saddlebag Lake Campground. Above south shore of Saddlebag Lake.

Resorts

Tuolumne Meadows Lodge. See the chapter "The Camps" for information.

Tioga Lodge. On Highway 120 just 300 yards south of Saddlebag Lake Road junction. Cabins, meals, food, fishing gear, gasoline.

Saddlebag Lake Resort. Above south shore of Saddlebag Lake. Meals, food, fishing gear, fishing license, boat rental.

Other Services and Activities

Tuolumne Meadows Store. Just west of entrance to Tuolumne Meadows Campground. Food, supplies, fishing gear, fishing license, cafe, post office. Gas station nearby.

Tuolumne Meadows Stable. From Lembert Dome parking lot drive west 1/3 mile, then north ¼ mile. Offers ½-day, 4-day and 6-day rides. Phone (209) 372-4372. See the chapter "The Camps" for address.

Information Center. At entrance to Tuolumne Meadows Campground. Leave messages here.

Nature walks. Check at Information Center.

Field seminars. In-depth courses by qualified instructors. Phone (209) 372-4532. Address: Yosemite Natural History Association, P.O. Box 545. Yosemite National Park, CA 95389.

Mountaineering instruction. See the chapter "Climbers."

Boating. In the Park, only on Tenaya Lake in this quadrangle. Nonmotorized boats only.

Hang gliding. Usually at Glacier Point; check with Park Headquarters for flying elsewhere.

Nearest town. Lee Vining, 13 miles north of Tioga Pass.

Lyell Fork by the footbridge

RECOMMENDED READING

Adams, Ansel and Virginia, *Illustrated Guide to Yosemite.* San Francisco: Sierra Club, 1963.

Bailey, Edgar H. (ed.), *Geology of Northern California.* Sacramento: California Division of Mines and Geology, 1966.

Basey, Harold E., *Sierra Nevada Amphibians.* Three Rivers, CA: Sequoia Natural History Association, 1969.

Farquhar, Francis P., *History of the Sierra Nevada.* Berkeley: University of California Press, 1965.

Hill, Mary, *Geology of the Sierra Nevada.* Berkeley: University of California Press, 1975.

Horn, Elizabeth L., *Wildflowers 3: The Sierra Nevada.* Beaverton, OR: Touchstone Press, 1976.

Hubbard, Douglas, *Ghost Mines of Yosemite.* Fresno: Awani Press, no date.

Ingles, Lloyd G., *Mammals of the Pacific States.* Stanford: Stanford University Press, 1965.

Muir, John, *The Mountains of California.* Garden City, NY: Doubleday, 1961.

Peterson, P. Victor and P. Victor, Jr., *Native Trees of the Sierra Nevada.* Berkeley: University of California Press, 1975.

Roper, Steve, *The Climber's Guide to the High Sierra.* San Francisco: Sierra Club, 1976.

Stebbins, Cyril A., and Robert C., *Birds of Yosemite National Park.* Yosemite National Park: Yosemite Natural History Association, 1974.

Storer, Tracy I., and Robert L. Usinger, *Sierra Nevada Natural History.* Berkeley: University of California Press, 1963.

Thomas, John H., and Dennis R. Parnell, *Native Shrubs of the Sierra Nevada.* Berkeley: University of California Press, 1974.

Weeden, Norman F., *A Sierra Nevada Flora.* Berkeley, Wilderness Press. 1981.

Zwinger, Ann H., and Beatrice E.Willard, *Land Above the Trees.* New York: Harper & Row, 1972.

Tuolumne Meadows

Index

Trail Notes

Trail Notes

Conservation organizations

The price of wilderness, like liberty, is eternal vigilance. Someone is always about to carve off a piece of wilderness to use for tree cutting, mining, ski resorts or something else. If you always want to have nice places to go backpacking, you'll have to expend a little effort to help save these places. Fortunately, there are a number of existing organizations that are already set up to work for wilderness. They simply need your help.

I urge you to get in touch with any or all of the organizations listed below, and join the ones that seem best to you.

Appalachian Mountain Club
5 Joy St.
Boston, MA 02108

The Mountaineers
719 Pike St.
Seattle, WA 98101

American Hiking Society
18600 S.W. 157th Ave.
Miami, FL 33187

National Parks and
   Conservation Association
1701 18th St. N.W.
Washington, D.C. 20009

California Wilderness
   Coalition
P.O. Box 429
Davis, CA 95616

Sierra Club
530 Bush St.
San Francisco, CA 94108

Friends of the Earth
124 Spear St.
San Francisco, CA 94105

The Wilderness Society
1901 Pennsylvania Ave.
Washington, D.C. 20006

—Thomas Winnett, President
Wilderness Press